D1171077

The Tears of War

The Tears of War

Ingeborg E. Ryals

iUniverse, Inc.
Bloomington

The Tears of War

iUniverse books may be ordered through booksellers or by contacting:

iUniverse
1663 Liberty Drive
Bloomington, IN 47403
www.iuniverse.com
1-800-Authors (1-800-288-4677)

ISBN: 978-1-4759-3273-7 (sc)
ISBN: 978-1-4759-3275-1 (e)
ISBN: 978-1-4759-3274-4 (dj)

Library of Congress Control Number: 2012910871

Printed in the United States of America

iUniverse rev. date: 9/12/2012

This book is dedicated to the innocent victims of World War II. It was a war that spanned several continents and touched the lives of many. They endured hardships, starvation, and untold atrocities at the hands of others, often paying the ultimate price. To honor their memory, let us strive to make this a better world in which one is not judged by nationality, race, or religion but by the kindness and compassion one shows toward his fellow man. Let us rise above the use of force and solve our differences in a more humane and civilized way so another war of such vast proportions will never again touch our lives.

FOREWORD

In the early seventeenth century, the land of Pomerania was for the most part covered with virgin forests. Untouched by man, large stands of beech and oak trees spread out across the landscape. With the abundance of firewood, a small glass-producing plant was built in the year 1707.

Glass was a much sought-after commodity in those early days. It was a risky undertaking in this harsh and unforgiving environment. Some parts of the land were only accessible during the months of winter when the ground was frozen, or during the dry summer months. Without the aid of machinery, or any type of mechanical devices, the work was hard on man and beast. Large trees had to be felled by hand, and then transported by horse-drawn wagons to the plant where the wood was used in the glassmaking process. The wagons were often bogged down in the marshy terrain.

With the fires burning day and night, the logging operation ultimately took its toll on the forest. Where once tall, stately trees stood, only a wasteland of stumps and shrubs remained. Eventually the distance between the plant and the forest increased to such an extent that it became an unprofitable venture and it finally closed its doors.

Some of the workers left the area, while others decided to settle down, become colonists, and make this their permanent home. In exchange for land, the settlers agreed to clear the land and transform it into useable farmland. Over time, little villages sprang up all over the countryside surrounded by meadows and fields, with the edge of the dark forest still visible in the distance. Customs and traditions emerged forging a special bond between the different villages.

My grandfather's family settled in this region in 1732. He ran a blacksmith shop on the bank of the little Zarow River, which marked the boundary between two villages. It also was a regular stop for the stagecoach, which delivered the mail. After changing horses at his shop, the driver was soon on his way again. The blacksmith shop and the house are long gone now, along with the people who once lived there so many years ago.

PROLOGUE

There once was a land of green meadows and blue lakes; of fields where seas of wheat and rye swayed to the rhythm of the summer winds; and of dark forests where the wild boar, the doe, and the stag roamed. This was the home of my ancestors, where in the 1930s I spent the happy, carefree years of my childhood.

Our village in Pomerania, a province in northern Germany, was small, with tidy homes and well-kept yards. Most of the dwellings were single-story homes built of brick or stone, some still with thatched roofs while others had the newer shingled ones. In the summer months, each front yard was a sea of flowers surrounded by a stone or picket fence. The one and only street winding through the village was lined on both sides with large chestnut trees. In spring, when the trees were in bloom, it was a beautiful sight.

With the population only around a hundred, our village was far too small to support a church or any type of store. Mostly on weekends, we walked or bicycled to a much larger village less than a mile away to do our shopping at a variety of stores. Two large ballrooms held dances on weekends and even occasionally showed a movie. There was a foundry where some of the local men worked and a busy railroad station where numerous trains stopped daily on their way to and from Berlin. For the children, it was always a day of fun when walking through the village and snacking on ice cream and candy.

As for the people, they were a hardy breed, proud and hardworking, with perhaps a streak of stubbornness about them. The majority of them were farmers, while a few men worked outside the village at different jobs to provide for their families. They were God-fearing, but for them it was still "an eye for an eye" in this predominately Protestant region of the country. Somewhat superstitious, they strongly held on to the belief that shortly after death the deceased would return one last time to assure the family that all was well in the afterlife. It might be in the form of a shadow or an unexplained knock at one's door. The residents spent many long winter evenings telling old wives' tales by the flickering light of an oil lamp, with knitting needles clicking softly in the background and children listening intently, hanging on to every word. It was a simple but good life.

For the children, it was a time of laughter, running through the meadows trying to catch a butterfly and swimming in a nearby creek or riding home from the fields high atop a wagon loaded with fragrant hay. As summer turned into fall, it was time to harvest what had been sown in the spring. The threshing machines were humming day in and day out while separating the grain from the chaff. Soon the fields were barren and the colors of autumn spread their beauty across the land. A nip was in the air as nature once again prepared itself for the onslaught of winter.

The winter months were spent skating on a nearby pond or building castles of snow with passageways and courtyards. There was a snow queen and her court regally ordering everyone around. But as soon as the warmer winds of spring began to blow, our castles went by the way of the wind and all that was left were dirty heaps of snow.

As the days grew warmer, the miracle of spring once again unfolded, painting the barren landscape a light green. It was time to plow the land and plant the seeds for the next harvest.

In the summer of 1939, to celebrate my tenth birthday my mother surprised me with a weekend trip to one of the beautiful resorts along the Baltic Sea. A lighthearted atmosphere prevailed and the resorts were doing a booming business.

We took a swim in the ocean and strolled along the promenade where dance halls and cabarets were packed with fun-seeking crowds.

While everyone was dancing to the latest tunes or swaying to the rhythm of a Vienna waltz, war clouds were slowly gathering on the horizon. Rumors of war had been circulating for some time, when suddenly in September of 1939 German troops crossed the Polish border in a surprise attack known as the blitzkrieg. It marked the beginning of World War II, and overnight the party was over.

CHAPTER 1

The beginning of the war brought few changes to our way of life. We continued to work the land, celebrate weddings, welcome the birth of a child, and send the deceased off on their last journey. But gradually we were beginning to feel the effects of the war as it began to encroach upon and change our way of life. Daily, the radio programs were repeatedly interrupted with special reports that brought us the latest news bulletins from the front lines, recounting the victorious feats of our troops. At day's end, the station always concluded its broadcast with a popular vocalist, Lale Anderson, singing "Lili Marlene" in her deep, throaty voice. It was a very nostalgic song that was reminiscent of the time. It was the song of a soldier late at night bidding his ladylove good-bye, under a lamppost in front of his casern, before going off to war. She promises to wait at the same place, same time, under the lamppost for his return.

It was my mother, Anna's, favorite song. Every evening she listened to it faithfully before turning off the radio and retiring for the night. She was a slender woman with fine facial features and was of medium height. Her shoulder-length hair was not one of her better features. It was very fine and did not take well to perms, which always left her hair in a somewhat frizzy state. I think she would have looked far more attractive if she had let her hair grow out, braided it, and gathered it up in a bun, but perms were all the rage then. Long, braided hair was on the way out. Therefore, my mother continued with her frizzy hairstyle. She had a mellow personality and was slow to anger, but if you really tried her patience, then her temperamental side emerged. Once when an ornery old neighbor provoked her to no end, she all but smacked him over the head with a broomstick.

Life in the village was a lonely one for her. Now in her thirties, on rare occasions she would attend a dance in one of the neighboring villages. It was a far cry from the big city life she had become accustomed to in her early twenties when she followed her older sister to Berlin. Neither of them had wanted to stay in the village and marry a farmer. Instead, both of them moved to the big city and went to work for an electronics firm.

She eventually met and fell in love with my father, a dashing army officer. I am sure she thought they would live happily ever after, but soon after I was born, her mother was diagnosed with stomach cancer, an incurable illness. Since there was no one to look after her needs, she volunteered to move temporarily back to the village to take care of her while my father, of course, had to stay with his army unit in Berlin. We traveled back and forth to see my father, but after my brother Kurt was born, the trips to Berlin became less frequent. My grandmother was bedridden by then and had to be cared for around the clock. By the time she passed away at home at the age of sixty-two, my mother almost devoted two years of her life to her mother's care.

The long separation ultimately took a toll on my parents' relationship. After seeing my father a few more times in Berlin, they separated and went their own ways. Though he continued to support us, we had very little contact with him. After the age of five, I saw very little of my father. My mother decided to stay on in the village where she had grown up. I guess it was of some comfort to live out her days among the people she had known all of her life instead of in the big city among strangers.

I am sure single motherhood was not the kind of life she had once envisioned, but life can be very unforgiving sometimes, and the choices we make while young tend to have far-reaching consequences.

At the age of thirty-six, her social life was very limited until she met a very nice young man named Ernst at a local dance. After a courtship of several months, they eventually got married. By the time their son Gerhardt was born, in January of 1941, Ernst had already been drafted at the age of thirty-nine and gone off to war. There was hardly an able-bodied man left in the village. Almost every man had been drafted. Some of them were wounded or missing in action, while others had lost their lives on the battlefield. Many people wore black those days, the color of mourning.

Ingeborg E. Vetter (Ryals), 1941
12 years old

Anna Vetter Hasselmann, 1928

Chapter 2

As the war continued, we were issued ration cards for certain commodities, but since we lived in a farm region, food was plentiful, especially fresh vegetables, meat, and dairy products.

The government brought in forced labor from countries occupied by our troops, mainly France, Russia, and Poland. We desperately needed help with our farm work since most of our men were off fighting this dreadful war. The farmer provided room and board, but the workers received no compensation. Since their movements were not restricted, they were allowed to mingle freely with their fellow countrymen on evenings and Sundays after work. They seemed to adapt well to their new way of life, even playing games with the local children in their free time; however, a few ladies in the next village were a little too friendly with the charming, good-looking Frenchmen and promptly had their locks shaved off as punishment. It was frowned upon for women to socialize with them on an intimate basis.

Most of our best horses were gone, confiscated by the government to replace those lost in battle. Usually on short notice, cavalry officers in their smart-looking uniforms and polished boots showed up at our village, where the farmers had been instructed to gather at the schoolhouse with their prized horses. The animals underwent a thorough examination before they were selected for military service. In the end, the farmers were left with a few sway-backed mares and young colts. It was a real hardship on them since most of the heavy work, like plowing and tilling the land, was still done by horse-drawn machinery.

It would even affect our little volunteer fire department, which solely consisted of a horse-drawn wagon outfitted with a large tank. Parallel handlebars were attached to each end of the tank. It was so antiquated that it still had to be manually operated. In teams of three, the men positioned themselves at the front and back end of the tank, taking hold of the handlebars and moving them in rapid succession up and down. This created sufficient pressure to force the water out of the tank and into the attached hose. Since the mayor had the only telephone in the village, each volunteer had to be notified individually in case of a fire. By the time they had all assembled, hitched the horses to the wagon, filled the tank with water, and rushed to the site of the fire, in most instances, the volunteers arrived to find the building already consumed by the flames. One tank of water was of little help in a roaring blaze.

Such was the case when lightning struck Herr Bock's barn. Since it was filled with hay and straw, the fire spread rapidly. All efforts failed to save the barn and its contents, including a large pig that Herr Bock was fattening up over the summer to butcher in the fall. Most of our fires were caused by lightning strikes in the summer months. The thunderstorms were often quite severe. At times, we could hear the rumbling of thunder throughout the night.

On the outskirts of the next village, rows of single-story barracks were constructed out of wood with concrete flooring. The buildings were in stark contrast to the quaint, old dwellings of yesteryear, many of them built of brick and stone and some still with thatched roofs. The little compound was soon swarming with college-age girls from all walks of life. The majority of them were city girls in their late teens or early twenties who were pressed into service by the government to help with the farm work. Upon arrival they were issued uniforms and had to adapt to a very regimented life. Their manicured, pampered hands were soon a sight from working days on end in the fields or doing the various chores the farmers required of them. It was a far cry from the sheltered life they had enjoyed in the city, but no one dared to complain. All of them did as they were told. Each farmer most likely had to relinquish part of his crop to compensate the government for the help that was rendered.

There was not much in the way of entertainment for the young people. Dancing was prohibited, but we occasionally walked to the next village to see a movie. Even with the ongoing war, some of the old traditions still endured, like Herr Boerner and his clarinet. Every year on the first of May, we were awakened in the early morning hours by the sounds of a clarinet. For Herr Boerner, our neighbor, it had been a long-standing tradition to get up at the crack of dawn, walk to the middle of the road, and serenade the villagers with a May Day song on his clarinet. He was a tall, husky man with slightly stooped shoulders and a weathered face that was lined with wrinkles. In his younger days, he played on weekends in a small band whenever there was a dance in one of the surrounding villages, while during the week he toiled from dawn to dusk on his small farm. Ever since I could remember, he played the very same tune every first of May, but time marches on and he was getting on in years. As with all things in life, everything comes to an end. Old customs fade away, and so eventually would Herr Boerner and his beloved clarinet.

One of the numerous meadows that dotted the landscape had been converted into a small airstrip where pilots from the German Luftwaffe practiced takeoffs and landings daily. At night, they usually converged on the local pubs to cap off the day with a few drinks. At times, the music and singing continued far into the night. They were often joined by some of the local girls who had to sneak out of the house to join the merriment while their strict, old-fashioned parents thought they were safely tucked away in their beds. With so many handsome airmen around, it was just too tempting for the girls to pass up an evening of fun and perhaps meet the love of their life.

CHAPTER 3

Hardly any of the residents in our village concerned themselves with politics. A few of the men, including the mayor and the teacher, belonged to the National Socialist German Workers' Party (Nazi Party). I think they joined more or less to pacify the party officials at county headquarters than out of loyalty to Hitler. We never saw them in their easily recognizable uniforms. The farmers would much rather spend their time talking about the weather, their livestock, or what their next harvest might yield. However, all boys and girls were required to join one of Hitler's youth groups (Hitler Jugend). Most young people worked on the family farm after school and had little time for meetings. However, when we did have a get together, it was, more of a social event than a party function. As children, we saw it as an excuse to play and have fun.

Once, at the age of twelve, I was asked to host a meeting at the local school. My mother baked a cake for the occasion, but the meeting soon took on a party atmosphere. It began by playing games of tag and chasing each other around the room, over and under desks, making so much noise that the teacher, whose living quarters adjoined the school, suddenly appeared at the door and gave us a good tongue-lashing. It was not much of a meeting, but all of us had a jolly good time. Once a year, in one of the neighboring villages, sporting events were held by the Hitler Youth. For the two-day event, we were housed in a farmer's barn and had to furnish our own food. There was a lot of camaraderie, but there also was a great deal of competition for the much sought-after medals that were handed out to the winners at the closing ceremonies.

Rumors of discrimination began to circulate against certain minority groups; primarily people of the Jewish faith became their target. In the neighboring village, where we did most of our shopping, a Jewish merchant owned and operated a successful textile store for many years. Everyone from the surrounding villages shopped at his store. All of us were stunned when we heard the news that one night someone had smashed the large display windows at his store. He and his family had lived peacefully among us for many years. They were a part of our community. In the past, I often saw their two teenage girls but was not personally acquainted with them. They always looked so well groomed and fashionably dressed. Soon after the store was vandalized, I never saw them again and often wondered what eventually happened to them. Also, while visiting my aunt in Berlin, I noticed Jewish people wearing the yellow Star of David on their clothing. It was sad to see a certain group of people ostracized for their religious beliefs and especially see each young child walking around with a big yellow star attached to his or her outer garments.

By the spring of 1944, the war was coming closer with each passing day as our troops were retreating on all fronts and, for the first time, the Soviet Army was becoming a real threat to our eastern provinces. By now, hardly anyone had not been touched by tragedy relating to this war.

Three young men, our neighbors, returned home injured, each having lost the use of a leg. Two others never returned home at all, and we did not know what ever happened to them. Their families were devastated at not knowing.

In May of 1944, we received the sad news that my twenty-three-year-old cousin, Herbert, an airman stationed in East Prussia, had perished in a plane crash along with the rest of his crew. He was on one of his last training flights when, for unexplained reasons, his plane exploded in midair, killing everyone onboard. His plane was manned with combat-ready crews that had just finished months of intense training. We were told that his body would not be sent home, but instead he would be buried in a military cemetery close to the air base. He was an only child and would be greatly missed by all of us.

Herbert Vetter, 1925

Herbert Vetter, 1944

CHAPTER 4

With the German army retreating, scores of young people were shipped to the eastern part of the country in June of 1944 to build trenches behind the front lines. It was like soldiers going off to war. Their departure was always a tearful one, especially for the parents. Having just turned fifteen, it would only be a matter of time before I was called. When the mayor appeared at our door a few days later, we knew that it was not a social call; it was my turn to go.

The next day I was on a train with a group of other young people heading toward the eastern part of the country. Despite the seriousness of our mission, which was mandatory, a somewhat lighthearted atmosphere prevailed. No one was fearful or apprehensive. Instead, in our naiveté we viewed it more as an adventure. For most of us, it was our first time away from home for any length of time. A few cigarettes were passed around. We took our first puffs and felt really grown up. Edith, the mayor's daughter and my friend, also had to go. We played together, went to school together, and at times got into trouble together. Now we embarked on a new adventure together.

It was late afternoon when we finally arrived at our destination and were immediately bussed to a large country estate in the eastern part of Pomerania near the Polish border.

The loft of a large barn would be our home for the next few months. The horses stabled below made the whole place reek of farm animals. Our mattress consisted of a one-foot layer of straw plus blankets we had brought from home to keep us warm. It was by no means luxurious, but for the time being it would have to do. The bathroom facility left a lot to be desired as well. Two beams were spread over an open pit: one to sit on and the other one, positioned somewhat higher and farther back, to serve as a back support. A privacy fence surrounded this makeshift arrangement, but there was no roof to shield us from the elements.

For personal hygiene, we had only a couple of outside faucets at our disposal. Mornings and afternoons, it was going to be bedlam when everyone had to line up to brush their teeth or wash off a day's worth of dust and perspiration.

After we settled in, we were ready to explore our new surroundings and were pleasantly surprised to discover a small lake within walking distance of the estate. After the long train ride, the water looked cool and inviting, but no one thought to bring a bathing suit along. Since the lake was partly surrounded by trees and there were only girls present, we all decided to go swimming *au naturel.* A shepherd with his flock of sheep passed by and stared at us in disbelief, probably wondering where all these young maidens suddenly had come from. After regaining his composure, he waved at us and continued on his way while we enjoyed a good laugh.

After the evening meal, we fell into a deep sleep. It had been a long day, and the wakeup call would be early the next morning.

We ate a quick breakfast and then were trucked to different work sites. It never once crossed my mind that one day I would be standing here and digging trenches behind the front lines for our military. As I looked across the landscape—the meadows and the fields of wheat and rye—it all looked so deceivingly peaceful. After a soldier handed me a shovel, I asked him in a rather skeptical tone of voice, "How do you expect us to dig miles and miles of trenches with just a shovel in our hands?" He curtly replied, "One shovel at a time."

We soon learned that the trenches had to be 1.5 meters deep and eighty centimeters wide. Every few meters we had to dig a half circle into the side of the trench and leave up to thirty centimeters of soil at the bottom. Once the soldier stepped onto this elevated ledge, he had a lot better view of the surrounding area. It never failed. Every time I jumped into a trench and started digging, I was overcome with sadness. In all likelihood, blood would be shed and people were going to die in these very trenches. Perhaps my imagination was working overtime, but the future certainly did not look rosy. I hated this awful war; it had already touched and changed so many lives forever.

Physically we were by no means conditioned for this hard and strenuous work. It was taxing on body and mind. After just a few days, every bone in my body ached. I hated to get up in the early morning hours to face another day of hard labor. Sometimes at night, I cried softly into my pillow. I just wanted to go home. Without gloves, my hands were soon covered with blisters. A medic put some salve on my sore hands and bandaged them up, but the work had to go on so it was right back into the trenches.

On hot summer days, the sun was beating down on us mercilessly. Some of our fellow workers collapsed from heat exhaustion and sheer fatigue. After being revived, they were allowed a short rest before they had to go back into the trenches, where it was stiflingly hot and no cooling breezes would reach them. On rainy days, the water collected and puddled in the trenches. At times, we stood up to our ankles in mud while trying our best to shovel out the now much heavier dirt. But we were by no means mistreated; we all knew the work had to go on no matter how tired or fatigued we were.

We were finally getting a so-called *roof* for our toilet. A few tarpaulins were spread over the top and secured with ropes to keep the winds from blowing them away. To our horror, we discovered that we had an audience all along. A group of French farm laborers living in the barn directly above our bathroom facility had a front-row seat and watched our comings and goings. A girl happened to glance up one day and, to her dismay, saw at least a dozen pairs of eyes staring at her from above. So much for privacy.

After several weeks of hard labor, I was reassigned to kitchen duty. They discovered that I was only fifteen and consequently too young to work out in the fields. Anyone under sixteen should have been automatically assigned to kitchen duty. I had been assigned by mistake to work in the trenches. My new job involved peeling potatoes, cleaning vegetables, climbing into huge kettles, and scrubbing them with long-handled brushes until they were squeaky clean, plus endless washing of dishes and utensils. I vowed that I would never eat again. The food consisted mainly of one-dish meals like soups and stews, a nutritious but very monotonous fare.

The days went by ever so slowly. Summer turned into fall, and the nights were beginning to be quite cold. There was no heat, so at bedtime we burrowed a little deeper into the straw to keep warm.

The Soviet Army was coming closer with each passing day. They were fast approaching our eastern borders. It was all so very frightening and inconceivable to me. By now, the landscape was a labyrinth of trenches. Soon these would become the killing fields where many a brave young man would fight his last battle, and the trenches we dug would ultimately be his final resting place. One grows up awfully fast under these circumstances. This certainly was not the great adventure we had envisioned at the start of our journey.

Finally, on October 11, 1944, the order came that we could go home. We were so relieved and happy. We missed our families and all the comforts of home.

The return trip was quite different. The joviality and laughter were gone. We were a bedraggled and somber-looking lot, quietly sitting in our seats with everyone lost in his or her own thoughts. We were fearful of the future and the uncertain times ahead.

It was long after dark when the train pulled into the station. I was totally taken by surprise to see my mother and cousin Lorchen waiting to welcome me home, since no one had known the time or date of my return. In the past, they had made the mile-long walk to the station numerous times in hopes that I would return from the east on one of the special trains that brought workers home daily.

We had so much to talk about. I learned that my stepfather, Ernst, was missing in action and presumed dead on the eastern front—another casualty of this dreadful war. In all probability, he lost his life somewhere in Russia. Consequently, there was little hope that his remains would ever be recovered. He never was home long enough for us to establish a close relationship, but I felt so sad for my mother, who once again had to raise a child without its father. This was not the happy homecoming I had hoped for, but unfortunately, suffering is part of the journey of life. And I guess sooner or later all of us got our share of it. This, too, would pass as we tried to go on with our lives.

Chapter 5

Since my return, the air raid sirens were wailing intermittently day and night, rousing us time and again out of a sound sleep. We dressed hurriedly and joined other villagers out on the dark street. First, we detected a faint hum in the distance, which soon escalated into a loud roar as wave after wave of enemy planes passed overhead on their way to the port city of Stettin, near the Baltic Sea. Soon, searchlights swept across the sky and a deep rumble filled the air as the planes dropped their deadly cargo. I felt for the many people who would lose their lives and wondered how many planes would not return from their mission. This scenario repeated itself day in and day out. We became so accustomed to the sirens and the planes that, at times, we ignored them altogether and went on with the task at hand or turned over in bed to get a few more winks of sleep. After all, our village was a very unlikely target.

Christmas of 1944 passed quietly. With the world in turmoil all around us, it was hard to be in a festive mood. My family did bake a few cookies though, decorated a tree, and exchanged some small gifts. My mother's sister, Eliese, visited for the holidays. She always came laden with gifts for everyone. She was like my second mother, and I called her affectionately Tante Lieschen.

Even though they were sisters and deeply cared for each other, their personalities differed greatly. Tante Lieschen, being the older sister, was the more dominant one while my mother was of a somewhat passive nature. Tante always took charge of the household as soon as she arrived. The first few days usually passed without incident, but if they were together for any length of time the visit invariably ended in an argument after my mother finally had her fill of Tante Lieschen's controlling and bossy nature. On numerous occasions, Tante Lieschen packed her bags in a huff and took the next train back to Berlin. But they never stayed mad at each other for long. The argument was soon forgotten when a card arrived in the mail a few days after her hasty departure to let us know that she had arrived safely and had enjoyed her visit.

This holiday visit went well for a change. As the time of her departure approached, she asked me to return with her to Berlin for a short visit. As much as I wanted to go, my mother would not hear of it. She insisted that the city was under siege, bombarded day and night with heavy loss of life. She feared for my safety, but we begged, pleaded, and begged some more until she finally relented.

For me, Berlin was always an exciting place to visit. It was a very sophisticated city with its opera houses, theaters, wide boulevards, and beautiful architecture. For a fifteen-year-old girl, it was a nice change every so often from the quiet and simple country life.

Our trip by train was interrupted twice by air raids, which delayed our arrival considerably. It was late in the evening when we finally pulled into the station. The city, usually bathed in light, was dark and ominous looking. Once bursting with activity, the streets were now empty and deserted as few people ventured out at night anymore.

Early the next morning, my aunt, who had an apartment in the heart of the city, had to report for duty at the local post office. Every available man had been drafted so women were pressed into service to fill the big void left in the workforce. They delivered the mail, drove trucks, operated streetcars, and generally performed all the tasks necessary to keep the factories running and provide the essential services to the greater metropolitan area of Berlin.

There was so much death and destruction all around. Historical landmarks, churches, and row after row of apartment buildings now lay in ruins. It was sad to see this once beautiful city under siege and destroyed by the daily bombing raids.

While my aunt was at work, I took in all of the latest movies. One movie in particular made me forget this awful war for a couple of hours. The scenery was breathtaking. There was music, dancing, and romance. I did not want it to end, ever, but an air raid quickly brought me back to the real world. We had had more than our share of them lately. A good night's sleep was hard to come by anymore. Practically every cellar became a designated air raid shelter. During an attack, I ducked into the nearest one wherever I happened to be. They were usually crowded with old men, women, and children; all of us hoped and prayed that we would be spared, for very few shelters could withstand a direct hit. I stayed amazingly calm through all of this upheaval and had yet to experience any real fear, unlike the Berliners who had dealt with this on a daily basis for months. Perhaps my country upbringing had prepared me well for these stressful times.

The food rations in the city were still adequate, but if we wanted a little extra meat, vegetables, or butter then we had to go directly to the farmer and trade precious clothing or household goods for food. The authorities frowned on this practice, but so far they had tolerated it.

To replenish our food supply, my aunt, after finishing her shift at the post office, was leaving late in the afternoon to visit a few of the outlying farms in hopes of securing some dairy and meat products. With the transportation system in such disarray from the constant bombings, she probably would not return until tomorrow. I would be home alone for the evening and perhaps for the entire night.

After taking in a movie, I returned to the warm, cozy apartment and looked forward to a late-evening snack. As I was about to sit down with a good hot cup of freshly brewed tea, the still of the night was shattered once more by the shrill sound of air raid sirens. Out in the hall, people were soon scurrying down to the shelter, but with my aunt away, I decided to stay in the apartment, enjoy my cup of tea, and hope for the best. I really dreaded going down into the cellar. Once the heavy steel door clanged shut behind us, I felt like I was in a tomb. The air was stale and musty as we sat side by side in silence, often for hours at the time.

Loving classical music, I put Beethoven's Fifth Symphony on the record player and turned up the volume to drown out the noise of the exploding bombs as they rained from the sky. After what seemed like an eternity, the air raid was finally over, and once more, we had escaped with our lives. My aunt returned with food the next morning, and life went on in the besieged city.

It seemed that, with each passing day, the bombing raids were becoming more numerous. One night we had such a close call that my aunt feared for my safety. She decided that I would have to return home immediately.

We had already retired for the night when we heard those dreadful sirens once again. We hurriedly dressed, gathered up a few belongings, and rushed down into the cellar as the bombs began to fall all around us. We sat there impassively, listened, and waited as the minutes slowly ticked away.

Fraulein Ziemke, an old maid, was nervous and fidgety. She was so frightened that it was hard for her to sit still. The daughter of wealthy parents who owned a distillery, she had never married and was all alone now. A small child, having been roused from a sound sleep, was cross and whimpering when suddenly pandemonium broke loose. A shrill whistling sound filled the air, followed seconds later by a terrible, ear-shattering explosion. The building shook and the lights went out as a shockwave propelled us against the wall. We were engulfed in a cloud of dust. It was gritty and tasted of concrete. The little ones were screaming in terror and the old people were dazed and confused as we tried to make our way, coughing and choking, out of the cellar.

Once on the outside, a heavy cloud of acrid smoke hung over the area, making it difficult to breathe. Every windowpane was broken, covering the ground with shards of glass. There was some structural damage to our apartment building, but the adjoining one was totally destroyed. It was a direct hit. Once swarming with life and children's laughter, all that remained was a smoldering heap of rubble. There were no survivors. The roof of our building caught on fire, but since there was no help available, we hurriedly formed a bucket brigade to extinguish the flames. The bombardment continued as we feverously poured bucket after bucket of water on the smoldering fire until we finally managed to extinguish it.

From the rooftop, we had a good view of the city. Many buildings were on fire with flames leaping and dancing eerily out of windows. It truly was a frightening sight.

Covered from head to toe with dust and soot, we tried to make our way through the rubble back to our apartment, ever so thankful to have survived the attack. Everything was littered with debris. Some of the inside walls had collapsed, and every pane of glass in the apartment was broken. Totally exhausted, we cleared the debris off the beds and crawled in without bothering to clean up or even change our clothing.

By the first light of day, rows of corpses were lined up on the sidewalk, ready to be picked up by the undertaker. I saw the young, the old, and ladies in expensive fur coats. All of them were innocent victims of this war.

It was time to say my good-byes. With a heavy heart, I left the city that held so many happy memories for me. The Berlin

I loved was no more and would never be the same again. It was with great sadness that I said good-bye to my beloved aunt at the train station. We both knew that we might be parting for the last time. I had to return home to face the uncertain and frightening prospects of the invasion of our land by foreign soldiers, and she would continue to struggle for survival as the terrible bombing continued.

On the way home, the train was crowded, and the weather was sunny and clear. Those days it was better to travel on cloudy days or under cover of darkness. On clear days, a moving train was an easy target for enemy planes.

An old, grandfatherly man in a smart officer's uniform slowly paced up and down the aisle, visibly upsetting the lady seated next to me. Finally, she could not contain her anger any longer and shouted at him, "Who do you think you are, old man, strutting around here like a peacock? Take off your disgusting uniform and go home. Hitler and his Third Reich are finished. It is over." Surprised and somewhat taken aback by her outburst, he stared at her in disbelief but chose not to reply to her angry remarks. He turned sharply on his heel and walked away, while she settled back into her seat, obviously relieved that she had had her say. Up until now, I had not heard anyone dare to openly criticize Hitler, the military, or the Third Reich. I guess it was an indication of the changing times; people were finally not afraid to speak their mind.

The rest of my journey passed without further incident, and I was truly relieved when the trip was finally over.

Everyone at home was eager to hear firsthand about the latest developments in the capital. The news I brought back was not encouraging. It only added to their fear and anxiety, but I had to be truthful about a great city in ruins, its many innocent victims, and a war that seemed all but lost.

(Tante) Aunt Lieschen Vetter

(Tante) Aunt Lieschen Vetter

Chapter 6

The freezing cold that plagued us this winter persisted as January turned into February. Coal, our primary source of fuel, was rationed and our supplies were running low. To heat our homes, we still used old-fashioned tile ovens. Early each morning, we built a roaring wood fire to which the coals were added later. All day long, the tiles radiated heat into the room, keeping it toasty and warm even on very cold days. To conserve coal, we only heated one room in the house. In other parts of our home, it was so cold that ice crystals formed on the walls. There were days I hated to get out of bed and usually waited until the fire was lit in the oven before getting dressed.

The bad news from the front continued. Our troops were suffering heavy losses. Supplies were not reaching them, and many of our men were facing starvation and freezing to death. The Soviet troops were pushing deeper into Germany's heartland, leaving a trail of death and destruction in their path. I guess the trenches we built were not much of a deterrent. So much for all the hard work.

In a last desperate attempt to save his Reich, Hitler recruited the few remaining men—the old and the very young—to fight his hopeless war. It was pure madness to send this ragtag group of untrained civilians up against the mighty Soviet Army.

Refugees from the eastern provinces of East Prussia, Silesia, and Pomerania began to pass through our villages, their belongings piled high on bicycles, carts, and horse-drawn wagons. After being on the road for weeks, they were exhausted and hungry. All the things we took for granted, such as a hot bath and brushing one's teeth, they had to do without. It was especially hard on the little ones. Many of them could not endure the hardships and died along the way. If time allowed, they were hurriedly buried in makeshift graves. Every refugee had a horror story to tell of Russian soldiers running amok, raping, plundering, killing, and committing unbelievable acts of violence against the civilian population, adding credence to similar reports that had been circulating for some time. It left me with an uneasy feeling that I could not seem to shake.

For days now, we were busy peeling potatoes, scrubbing vegetables, and preparing large kettles of soup to feed the starving refugees. After a good meal and a little rest, they were on their way again, trying to put as much distance as possible between themselves and this brutal enemy.

CHAPTER 7

As March of 1945 approached, we were busy with the confirmation for my brother, Kurt. Even with the enemy practically at our doorsteps, the church in the next village planned to go ahead with the religious ceremony, which was an important event in these young people's lives. At fourteen, it marked the end of their formal education. Most of them would stay at home and work on the family farm while others would learn a trade or, if their parents could afford it, leave for the city to further their education at an institute of higher learning.

The proper attire for this solemn occasion was a dark suit for boys while the girls were dressed entirely in black. For all of them, it marked the end of an era, the end of their carefree childhood years.

Finding a proper suit for my brother was almost impossible. My mother spent endless hours checking every clothing store in the area without success. My aunt, hearing of our search, was finally able to locate one in Berlin. We would have to go by train to meet her at a station midway to the city to pick up the much sought-after suit.

When we arrived at the designated station, it was crowded with refugees occupying every available space. They were sprawled on benches and tables or squatting on floors and were surrounded by the few belongings they were able to carry. Fear and apprehension were etched on their faces. They were the innocent victims of this war, now homeless with no place to go, having fled from the eastern provinces one step ahead of the invading Soviet Army.

Ours was but a short visit. With refugees everywhere, there was not a table or chair to be had for a quick cup of coffee or sip of lemonade. Also, it was very unnerving to hear the muffled sounds of heavy artillery in the distance. It was close enough to rattle the windows and make the earth tremble.

After a tearful good-bye, we boarded our train and then headed in opposite directions, hoping this was not our final farewell.

On the last Sunday in March, the day of my brother's confirmation, the church was filled to capacity. The church, built in 1722, with its massive walls and leaded windows, had withstood the ravages of time. The brick floor, now hollowed out in places, was mute testimony to the many feet that trod across it in the last two centuries. The large angel suspended from the ceiling was always an object of awe and curiosity for me as a child. The old chapel had witnessed countless weddings and funerals, the joys and the sorrows of many generations past.

Throughout the ceremony, including the hymn singing and the pastor's prayers for peace on earth, we could hear heavy artillery pounding away in the distance. It was an ever-present reminder of the ongoing war, even in a house of worship. A small gathering at our home followed, but no one was in the mood to celebrate.

A few days later, we were notified that Kurt had to report for duty with the home guard (*Volksturm*). The unit he was assigned to was made up primarily of young boys with no military training. My mother was beside herself. Kurt was only fourteen and small for his age. But, of course, he had to comply or face the consequences. Also, she would not be able to keep in touch or know his whereabouts.

Lutheran Church, Ferdinandshof, Germany

Kurt Vetter, age 12

Ingeborg Vetter, Confirmation, 1943 L to R Gerda Bassow, Ingeborg Vetter, Edith Lutz

CHAPTER 8

By April, winter finally had lost its grip. Spring was in the air and the weather was a lot more agreeable. The air raids all but stopped. I guess the planes had done their job. Now the ground troops would deliver the coup de grace.

On the highway, a mile away, our tanks and heavy artillery were still heading toward the front lines. Day and night, we heard their noisy clatter. The young soldiers manning them were so very brave to face this formidable enemy—with no hope of victory but almost certain death. Their orders were to fight to the very end. Soldiers from other units were not quite as brave and started to desert, knowing that they were fighting a losing battle. These deserters were passing through our village, sleeping by day and traveling by night so they would not be caught, because deserters would promptly be executed. We fed, sheltered, and gave them civilian clothes, and then we burned their uniforms.

A girl in the village was seriously thinking of having a sexual encounter with one of the soldiers in hopes of getting pregnant by a German. She was terrified of conceiving a child from a brutal rape attack by enemy soldiers. My efforts to convince her that she may be spared fell on deaf ears. For someone who never even dated, she obviously was not thinking straight. Hopefully she changed her mind.

CHAPTER 9

The April weather took a turn for the worse. For days on end it was dark and cloudy with intermittent rain showers, while the nights were damp and cold. The rumble of artillery and mortar fire was beginning to sound like a continuous roll of thunder, but most frightening was the eastern sky after dark. A crimson glow reached high into the heavens like an inferno of immeasurable proportions. It was the most terrifying sight I had ever witnessed.

We were quite certain by now that it would be only days before the line of battle reached our area. A feeling of utter helplessness and despair prevailed as we gathered quietly in the street after dark. It was a still night, with no breeze rustling through the trees or a single star in the sky, as we tried to decide where to go and what to do during the invasion.

Some families wanted to pack up and head toward the American lines. Rumors had it that the Americans were far more civilized and humane. Some wanted to stay in the village and take their chances, while others wanted to take refuge in the forest. After much discussion, the majority chose the forest, while three families, including mine, decided to stay. I could not bear the thought of being left behind. There was a good chance that our village might be attacked and burned to the ground. I felt that we could hide from the enemy in the forest, but, no matter how much I begged and pleaded, my mother's mind was made up. We would stay.

The hour was late, but we continued to huddle in groups. Somehow, it was more comforting to stay close together and share with each other our thoughts, apprehensions, and fears.

Then, from the east, a faint, unfamiliar sound echoed through the night. We waited and listened. As it slowly grew louder, we realized that these were the anguished cries of hundreds of sheep and cattle. They had been gathered from farms and large country estates in the eastern provinces and were now being relentlessly driven westward with little food, water, or rest, just one step ahead of the enemy. It seemed that everyone had to pay a price in this dreadful war, even the poor animals.

The night was far gone, and we were about to return to our homes, when my brother Kurt came hurrying down the street. He was pushing a bike with some of his belongings draped over the handlebars. It was good to have him home. Whatever hardships, trials, and tribulations lay ahead, as long as we were together we could face them.

We learned that during the first two weeks after being drafted, his unit was made to dig trenches. Then they made a long march to the nearest military installation for basic training and instruction in warfare. Soon thereafter, word leaked out that the Soviet Army had broken through the German defense line, crossed the Oder River, and was advancing rapidly toward them. They were ordered to burn and destroy everything in their path. In the panic and confusion that followed, Kurt was able to make his escape unnoticed, knowing that a few teenage boys were not going to stop the mighty Soviet Army. Every bridge crossing was heavily guarded, but having changed into civilian clothes and looking young for his age, he was able to pass without being challenged. We certainly were relieved to have him home.

There were so many last-minute things to do before the invasion. In the cellar, we would have to prepare a supply of food, enough to last us up to several weeks. God help us if the enemy found it, for without food we could not survive.

Herr Kopelmann, a merchant in the next village, where we had been shopping for many years, was asking everyone to come and help himself or herself to the food that was left on the shelves of his store. He would much rather give it to his customers than let it fall into the hands of the enemy. We gladly accepted his kind offer and got our fair share.

After the food was safely stored away, we packed our valuables into a large, solid-oak trunk made by my grandfather many years ago. With the help of neighbors, we buried the trunk deep into the ground of our vegetable garden. Even the featherbeds were packed away. So from now on, we slept on bare mattresses.

Everyone in the village was busy burying his or her possessions, for we were told that the enemy soldiers would steal anything in sight. They were especially fond of watches.

Herr Kopelmann's store

Chapter 10

Daily, the line of battle was drawing closer. We heard from retreating German soldiers that the enemy would reach us in two or three days. In some of the surrounding towns and villages, people were beginning to commit suicide. Many families chose death rather than falling into the hands of this dreaded enemy.

We did not sleep regular hours anymore. Fully clothed, we took occasional naps, as the rumble of artillery fire grew louder with each passing day. At night, the eastern sky was still aglow with the many fires that accompanied this war.

By April of 1945 we knew it was time to evacuate, so those planning to leave set their departure for the next day.

Dawn came early in the northern hemisphere. By the first light of day, the village was buzzing with activity as the horse-drawn wagons were hurriedly loaded and piled high with food, bedding, and various household items. Should their homes be burned to the ground, they would have at least saved some of their belongings.

By noon, the evacuees were present and eager to leave. The whips were cracking as the horses strained under their heavy loads, slowly setting the wagon train in motion. Soon they were out of sight and on their way to the forest, while I was left standing in the middle of the road. I had never felt so alone. As I looked around me at the empty homes and the deserted street, with not another living soul in sight, I totally lost my composure. I could not and would not stay one moment longer. I had to go and follow the others to the forest. All of the horror stories we had heard repeatedly over the past months from the fleeing refugees—of women being raped and people being robbed of their possessions—left me in a state of sheer terror as the minutes ticked away and I was about to come face-to-face with this feared enemy. The unthinkable was now happening: the fast-approaching Soviet Army was practically at our doorstep.

I rushed past my mother and into the house, grabbed a blanket, and threw a few belongings into a bag. Also, I needed a large, white handkerchief to wave at the enemy in a show of surrender. Kurt stared at me in disbelief, probably wondering what had come over me. Usually quiet and reserved by nature, I was totally out of control and acting in an irrational manner, but he did not interfere or attempt to stop me.

My mother tried to reason with me that we had no means of carrying our provisions like food, water, and blankets to the forest while we had easy access to our hidden food supply right below us in the cellar. Besides, she pointed out, there were plenty of places for young girls to hide in the village like attics, barns, or cellars rather than in the open forest. All of her attempts to dissuade me fell on deaf ears. She then physically tried to restrain me, but I pulled away and was out the door in a flash. Never before had I so blatantly disobeyed her, but the fear at that very moment was so great that nothing else mattered more than getting to the safety of the forest.

I ran as fast as my legs would carry me, stopping only long enough to pick up a branch to attach my white handkerchief flag to.

The road was clogged with people from other villages, and everyone was running from the enemy. A young German officer, incensed when he saw my white flag, grabbed it, broke the branch in two, and threw it to the ground while shouting, "There will be no surrender!" He acted as if he was going to take on the whole Soviet Army all by himself.

I had no trouble finding our little group camped out in a thicket of pine trees at the edge of the forest. My mother and two brothers followed later in the afternoon. She did not want me to face the upcoming ordeal alone and was not even angry with me for disobeying her. I felt a lot safer here in the company of the villagers and the sudden panic attack was all but gone.

At dusk, I walked with my older cousin, Lorchen, to the edge of the forest. A peaceful scene awaited us there. Cows were grazing in the meadow, and the windmill that for years had ground our wheat and rye was standing motionless at the edge of the creek. Tomorrow, everything would change. The Red Tide would engulf us all.

Sleep did not come easily as we bedded down for the night. It was cold and damp and the ground, covered with pine needles, was so hard that I could not get comfortable. Even the horses were restless. Usually stabled at night, they were stomping and pawing the ground. It was a night of tossing and turning. The fear and anxiety of what the next day would bring robbed many of us of sleep.

The long night finally ended, and the day that we had been dreading for so long was here. By the first light of day, I hurried to the edge of the forest to scan the eastern horizon, but all across the meadow a patchy fog hugged the ground, reducing visibility almost to zero. We had no water for freshening up or brushing our teeth, but these things become so insignificant in the face of adversity.

By eleven o'clock everyone was starting little campfires to cook their noon meals, giving little thought to the fact that the enemy might spot our smoke.

By eleven thirty our campsite was attacked; the battle had begun. Shrill, piercing sounds filled the air as artillery shells exploded all around us. Terrified, we ran deeper into the forest; women scooped up their little ones or dragged them along by their arms. We left everything behind as we ran for our lives. Suddenly, a burst of gunfire stopped us dead in our tracks. Someone shouted, "Down! Everyone down!" and instantly, we dropped to the ground. In our haste to escape the shelling, we almost ran head-on into a Russian army unit making its way through the forest. They were pinned down to the right of us by machine gunfire coming from a farmhouse occupied by German soldiers.

We were so close to the battle that bullets were whistling over our heads, hitting the trees above us. We pressed our bodies close to the ground and buried our faces in the musty smelling moss. My little brother, Gerdi, wedged between my mother and me, was ready to get up, thinking this was but a game. We physically restrained him and pushed his little head down repeatedly. Whimpering, he finally stopped struggling and resigned himself to the fact that he simply could not get up.

Suddenly, on command, the enemy soldiers were on their feet ready to attack. With their bone-chilling battle cry, "Ourrah, Ourrah," and bayonets poised, they pressed forward, only to be driven back to their original positions by a volley of machine gunfire from the farmhouse. They left their wounded and dying behind.

Again and again, they attacked and regrouped as the battle raged on and their casualties mounted. Finally, by midafternoon, they were on the attack once more. With bayonets in place and shouting their "Ourrahs," they managed to storm the farmhouse and the battle was over at last.

Slowly we got up, shaken to the core but thankful to be alive. Our faces were flushed and our clothes were in disarray as we made our way back to the campsite, with sporadic gunfire and the moans of the wounded and dying echoing across the battlefield.

Oh, how I hated this war! My eyes stung with tears as I thought of the pain, the suffering, and the terrible waste of young lives.

According to one of the wounded German soldiers, who survived by feigning death, the enemy showed no mercy toward the wounded and captured soldiers. They were promptly clubbed and bayoneted to death. Quite a few of them were teenage boys trying to defend their country.

After their gruesome deed, the Russian soldiers moved on to conquer what was left of the place that we called home.

At the campsite, we found everything still intact. Nothing had been ransacked or stolen. The fires had burned themselves out, with our half-cooked dinners still in the pots.

By late afternoon we had our first encounter with a Russian soldier. He approached our camp with a large automatic rifle casually slung over his shoulder and was pushing a bicycle. He was a boy of only eighteen or nineteen and had childlike, Slavic features; his uniform was far too large and ill fitting. He looked so poor that I almost felt sorry for him. A woman shouted, "He's got my bicycle!" But not understanding our language, he paid little attention to her remark. Through gestures, he indicated that he wanted to know the time. All of us obligingly pulled out and checked our watches only to have him walk over and snatch them unceremoniously from our hands. We could not say that we were not forewarned, but he looked so very young, not at all the type to be feared.

His booty was eighteen watches, some of them antique timepieces passed down from father to son. Once he was gone, we took stock of our jewelry. We removed rings, earrings, and necklaces and safely tucked them away.

We had heard so many horror stories of earrings being ripped out and fingers being cut off just because the person wearing them did not hand them over fast enough. For the girls, there was the ever-present threat of rape, so when a small group of soldiers approached our camp toward evening, Lorchen and

I were hurriedly covered with quilts and blankets. Lorchen's Uncle Anton, an invalid who had lost a leg in the war, flopped himself on top of us. He sat squarely on my back, making it difficult for me to breathe. It was extremely uncomfortable, but the alternative would have been far worse.

After foraging through the camp and taking things to their liking, the soldiers were on their way again.

All was quiet as we settled in for the night. For me it was a restless one, as I relived the past events in my dreams. The soldiers were screaming their "Ourrahs" once more, but this time they were coming at me from all directions with their gleaming bayonets poised and ready to strike. I was relieved when I woke up, still in one piece, and the night was finally over.

Herr Anton Saupe

CHAPTER 11

With the invasion over, we decided to go home; there was no need for us to stay any longer in the forest. We would be passing quite a few soldiers along the way, and to keep from being molested all the women and girls would have to wear a disguise. Some chose to wear men's clothing while others were going to dress as little old ladies. Some of the older women still wore ankle-length dresses and were willing to share them with us, so I decided to dress as a granny.

With the help of ashes, my face was made to look a dirty gray. An old-fashioned pair of spectacles was positioned on the tip of my nose, and to hide my blonde hair a triangle scarf was knotted tightly underneath my chin, and then pulled down to partially hide my face. A pillow, stuffed under my granny dress, gave me a well-rounded humpback look, and a cane made my outfit complete. I hardly recognized myself.

As we looked at each other dressed in these outlandish clothes, we got the giggles, resulting in a severe tongue-lashing from some of the older women. They reminded us that the predicament we were in was no laughing matter. Being very respectful of our elders, we tried our best to keep a straight face.

These disguises assured us safe passage to the village. Soldiers did not even give us a second look as we hobbled along the road with our canes, looking more like witches than sweet little old ladies do.

At the entrance to our village, we recognized dishes from my uncle's house scattered along the sandy road. There was evidence of fighting, but surprisingly there was very little structural damage to the buildings.

In our neighbor's front yard were five freshly dug graves of Russian soldiers, with crudely constructed wooden markers. Each was topped with a large red star, the color synonymous with communism. In a faraway country, someone would grieve and shed many tears for these fallen soldiers, but such was war.

Our home had been ransacked, with an array of broken dishes and household goods littering the floor, but the food in the cellar was left untouched and there was no damage to the building itself.

The families that stayed behind in the village fared much better than we did. A few of their belongings had been taken, but no harm had come to any of them. They reported that the advancing troops were fairly well behaved, and after securing the village they were eager to push on.

Our little redbrick, one-room schoolhouse was used as a makeshift operating room during the attack, with blood still covering the desks, the floor, and the white featherbeds gathered from nearby homes. There was much evidence of suffering. The soldiers buried in our village most likely spent their last moments of life here in this very room.

Chapter 12

Word reached us that there was a wounded man on the outskirts of the village, and he was bleeding from a gunshot wound but refusing all help. He wanted to die and asked to be left alone. Horst, a boy my age, and I volunteered to investigate, partly out of curiosity and partly in hopes of persuading him not to give up on life.

We found a distinguished-looking man, perhaps in his fifties, curled up in a fetal position in a mound of straw with blood slowly trickling from a wound to the upper part of his body. At first, he was annoyed and angry at our intrusion, pleading with us to leave him alone so that he could die in peace. But after a little prodding, he related to us in a weak and halting voice the events that led up to his present predicament.

Once a prosperous businessman from the city of Stettin, he had lost his family and his business in a bombing raid. After the Russians conquered the city, he was arrested and on his way to one of their infamous prisons. He managed to escape by jumping off a moving truck but was shot in the process and left for dead. Bleeding, and without food or shelter, he spent the night in a farmer's barn, but once discovered, the farmer, fearing retribution from the Russians for harboring an escaped prisoner, promptly ordered him off his property. Having lost his family and all of his worldly possessions, he also lost his will to live. Nothing we said or did changed his mind. Before we left, we covered him with straw to give him a little more protection from the elements and planned to check on him again.

The next day we returned with food and water, but there was no sign of him. His hollowed-out little shelter was empty, the straw still caked with his blood. We never knew his name, and after returning to the village, we learned that a man in a weakened condition and fitting his description was led away by soldiers. Perhaps his last wish would be fulfilled after all, for few survived the rigors of a Russian prison. Just another nameless person disappearing without a trace, never to be heard from again.

Chapter 13

Ever since the invasion, a smoky, acrid haze covered our region, stinging our eyes and throats and permeating every piece of clothing, our hair, and even our bedding. The air was so polluted that it totally obliterated the sun.

Life in the village was far from normal these days as we were beginning to live through some of the same horror stories told to us by the fleeing refugees. Undisciplined bands of drunken Russian soldiers raped, looted, and murdered their way to the front lines. Most of them showed no mercy and seemed to derive great satisfaction from subjecting us to their cruel and inhuman treatment.

My girlfriend was raped repeatedly as she and her family made their way from eastern Pomerania to our little village. At times, up to twenty soldiers stood in line and assaulted her repeatedly while her family stood helplessly by. If husbands or fathers tried to intervene, they had best say their last prayers, for the drunken soldiers did not take kindly to being deprived of their pleasure. At times, a woman was spared by repeating a phrase, coined out of necessity, "Madja krank, maschine kaput." That meant, "Woman is sick, machine broken," which implied that she was sexually dysfunctional or was infected with a venereal disease. It was a crude way of putting it and was often ignored by the soldiers. We were totally at their mercy and had no one to turn to for help or protection. The ones in command looked the other way and made no effort to intervene or assist us in any way. We had to be on guard around the clock and secure our own little world as best as we could. Young boys served as lookouts during the day, and whenever soldiers approached, the word was spread quickly throughout the village. Girls and women immediately dropped whatever they were doing and went into hiding.

Living across the street from Anton and his family, I usually took refuge in their house. It was larger than ours and had many good places to hide. I preferred the attic. From up above, I was able to watch the movements of the soldiers and could come out of hiding as soon as they were out of sight.

Not so when I took refuge in the field, the wheat being just high enough to conceal a person. At times, I would stay there for hours, afraid to venture out. Usually lying on my back, I watched the clouds drift slowly across the sky and wished I could float away on one to a safer and better world.

Once I had no choice but to hide out in the loft of a neighbor's barn filled with last year's harvest. Little mice were scurrying all about. Although I was deathly afraid of them, I could not let out a good healthy scream for fear of being discovered.

The safest but most confining place was a little closet beneath the stairs in Anton's house. Once the door was closed, a large wardrobe was pushed across it, effectively hiding the entrance. Sometimes alone, sometimes with cousin Lorchen, I spent many hours in this pitch-dark hideaway, often hearing soldiers' voices and footsteps as they rummaged through the house. It was especially scary when the soldiers examined the contents of the wardrobe directly in front of the closet door with only a few inches separating us. All kinds of awful thoughts would go through my mind. *What if they set the house on fire? There will be no way for me to escape!* The idea terrified me.

At times, I tried to dispel my fears by daydreaming, imagining myself far away on a beautiful tropical island with palm trees swaying softly in the breeze and the sound of waves gently lapping the shore. Or I was seated at a banquet table laden with every imaginable delicacy and eating to my heart's content.

At other times, I pretended that I was the belle of the ball, dressed in a most beautiful gown and swaying around the dance floor in the arms of a handsome young stranger. These little fantasies helped me to cope and transformed me temporarily into another world. It was always a relief when the wardrobe was finally moved aside and I was released from my dark, little hideaway.

Chapter 14

We dared not sleep in our homes at night, as roving bands of enemy soldiers might drop in unexpectedly. Every evening, we trudged across the street to Anton's house, where we, along with his family, hid in the feed room of his cow barn. It was a small room where daily rations of hay for the livestock were pitched down through an opening from the hayloft above. This little room became our refuge, where we could at least sleep undisturbed and without fear.

The first few nights were uneventful. It was the beginning of May and the hour was late when we were aroused out of a deep sleep by loud voices and a commotion outside. One look out of our little window confirmed our worst fears. We were surrounded by Russian soldiers.

With their rifles stacked nearby, and a large pig roasting over an open pit, the soldiers were milling all about. One in particular caught my eye. He was tall and dark complexioned, probably of Mongolian descent, and I thought, the scariest-looking human being I had ever seen. His cheeks were stuffed with food, and a few of his front teeth were missing, making it difficult for him to chomp down on a large piece of meat. The flickering light of the fire cast an eerie glow on this whole scene. Astonished, Lorchen and I looked at each other while remembering last New Year's Day when she rushed over to our house to tell us of a dream she had the night before.

In her dream, she described the very scene outside our window, almost in detail. Quite a few people still believed that dreams on New Year's Eve would come true. At the time, we tried to make light of it. We laughed and joked about the type of disguises we would wear to keep from being victimized. We even stuffed pillows under our clothes to achieve the hump-backed look and hobbled across the room with canes, never once expecting that some day it all would become reality.

In hushed tones, we tried to assess our situation but were totally at a loss as to what to do. Should we try to escape under cover of darkness and take the risk of being shot or stay in hiding until daylight and take our chances of not being discovered? With soldiers all around us, there would be no place to hide anyway. The minutes ticked away ever so slowly as we sat, waiting and worrying, wondering what the new day would bring.

As the first rays of light signaled the end of the night, a soldier appeared at our door. My mother, who was sitting slumped down in a corner of the room, hurriedly removed her false teeth and pulled a scarf down onto her face, trying to make herself look like an old woman. She mumbled in a low tone of voice, "There are no *madjas* here." The soldier glanced around the room and then left without a word, much to our relief.

After taking a look out the window, Anton, throwing all caution to the wind, was the first one to venture out. He could not stand idly by as the soldiers were defecating all over his property. The outhouse was out of order from overuse, with the soldiers nailing it shut permanently. Grabbing a shovel, he limped back and forth on his wooden leg, removing and burying the piles of human waste. The soldiers seemed to have no inhibitions. Whenever the urge overtook them, they relieved themselves wherever they were at the time, totally oblivious to anyone around them. Frightened, the rest of us huddled together in a corner of the room, not knowing what would lie in store for us.

Soon, Anton reappeared and assured us that we had nothing to fear and could come out of hiding. The Russian troops, on their way to the front lines, would be stationed in our village until further notice. Anton explained that, unlike the disorganized rabble bands that had passed through our village looting and raping, these soldiers were commanded by regular army officers who maintained strict discipline. Relieved, we scrambled to our feet shaking the hay out of our hair and clothing. Still somewhat apprehensive, Anton offered to escort us home. As we crossed the street, there were soldiers everywhere. A guard stationed at the entrance of our home blocked the way and would not let us pass. My mother was desperate; we had not eaten for some time, and all of our food was stored in the cellar of the house.

Through an interpreter, we learned that we needed written permission to enter our house and were asked to go directly to the recently established command post in the village. The officers there were of a different breed than the ragtag soldiers we had encountered so far. They looked clean, and their manners were much more civilized.

After obtaining the necessary document, we were back at the house and they finally allowed us to enter. Soldiers occupied almost every inch of our home. There was barely enough room to walk. Totally exhausted after a long march, they dropped wherever they were standing. One of them was even sleeping in Gerdi's baby bed, his legs dangling over the high railing of the crib. To our dismay, we discovered that the cupboards were empty and the provisions we had stored in the cellar were gone. Only empty bowls and jars remained, licked and scraped clean by the soldiers.

I had never seen my mother look so distraught and hopeless as we left our home. Tears were trickling down her cheeks as, for the first time in her life, she did not know how to feed her children. I tried to reassure her that all was not lost. The cows in the village were still giving milk and there were plenty of potatoes left, stored in underground beds. From now on, this most likely would be our diet morning, noon, and night. To make matters worse, we were without a home and might have to live in a barn with the animals.

By late afternoon, this problem was solved. A Russian interpreter informed us that the civilian population would be assigned to three of the twenty-four houses in the village. The Soviet Army would occupy the rest until further notice.

So with only the clothes on our backs and a few pillows and blankets, we moved into a small house, which the Dahms family for generations called home.

Frau Dahms, the patriarch of the family, was a short, stout woman in her eighties. Deep wrinkles lined her face from years of hard work, with many a day spent from morning until night working side by side with her husband in the fields. Her long, white hair was parted in the middle, pulled straight back, and then braided and gathered into a bun. Like most older women, she still wore the long, dark dresses of yesteryear and was never without her apron. A deeply religious woman, she was supposedly blessed with healing powers. I remember my mother telling me that when I was an infant I developed a stubborn rash on my chin, which soon turned bloody from constant scratching. The doctor prescribed ointments, which did little to remedy the situation. Every morning, my hands and the sheets of my bed were stained with blood. In desperation, my mother sought out Frau Dahms, who gave specific instructions as to the time and place for our meeting. The rendezvous had to take place during a full moon at a designated spot by a stream, where she performed the healing ritual. My chin did eventually heal without any scarring whatsoever.

Eight families, approximately twenty-four people, tried to crowd into her little home. For two of the families, the quarters were simply too confining so they chose to stay in the loft of her barn instead.

As night approached, and we ate our meager supper of boiled potatoes and milk, Frau Dahms called everyone together with a solemn, worried expression on her face. She chose her words carefully: "It has been called to my attention that the Russians have brought in some heavy artillery and are pointing it in our direction. Having herded us together in this house, I suspect that they will attack us sometime during the night. I want every family to stay close together so that if death comes you will be with your loved ones. May God be with all of us."

Never one to show much emotion, she wiped a tear from her eyes with her work-worn hand and then slowly rose and continued to go about her business.

The past was so stressful, but this new revelation really unnerved us. People gathered their loved ones around them, hoping for the best but fearing the worst as the hours ticked away ever so slowly. Occasionally, I dropped off to sleep, only to wake up with a start a short time later. It was the longest night I had ever spent.

As the first rays of light appeared on the eastern horizon, we breathed a sigh of relief. We were still alive. We had survived the night.

The morning began with more boiled potatoes. I was already so tired of them, but for the time being this fare would hold body and soul together.

Before noon, the troops assembled in the street for daily inspection and exercise. They were a pitiful-looking lot. Most of them appeared to be of Mongolian descent, with clean-shaven heads and ill-fitting uniforms. Quite a few of them were missing some of their front teeth, probably due to poor hygiene. While they marched up and down the street, they were making faces and sticking their tongues out at us. We had never seen such childish behavior in adults. It seemed that we had been invaded by hordes of crude and uncivilized human beings. It was all so unreal. If someone had predicted that this state of affairs would ever occur in our little village, we would have scoffed at them.

Chapter 15

One early afternoon, there was a burst of activity in the garden next door. Russian soldiers were unloading hundreds of freshly cut evergreen trees and planting them in rows to create walkways with a large square in the center. Once everything was in place, an officer appeared at our door wanting to know if there was anyone who played a musical instrument. They were planning to have a garden party. Since Anton played the accordion, he willingly volunteered his services. They also needed dancing partners. "Would the ladies of the house please join them this evening?" I guess that after months of fighting and roughing it, they were ready for a little merriment.

We really dreaded to go, not knowing what to expect, but we were under their control and they might not take kindly to our refusal. We were somewhat reassured since Anton would be there and our elders promised to keep a close eye on us and hopefully have us home by nine o'clock.

Five of us volunteered to go: Lorchen and her best friend, Ilse, both nineteen years of age; two women in their thirties; and myself, all of fifteen years old. We did not primp or fix our hair in order to look as unappealing as possible and trudged reluctantly next door in our old, everyday clothes. The officers, standing in a group, were awaiting our arrival. We kept a safe distance and eyed each other from across the square.

As Anton began to play, a handsome young officer asked me to dance. He was tall and blond and could easily pass for a fellow countryman. We did not speak each other's language, so there was little conversation as we danced the evening away. During the course of the evening, he also played a few tunes on the piano; apparently, he was an accomplished pianist himself. We were so grateful that all of them were sober and perfect gentlemen. But promptly at nine o'clock, we left our dance partners standing dumbfounded on the dance floor and disappeared into the night.

Later, as I drifted off to sleep, I relived the events of the day once more. What a strange turn of events. Here we were dancing and partying with the enemy, though not of our choosing. We had to do whatever was necessary to survive.

The sleeping arrangements at the Dahms house left much to be desired. Packed in there like sardines, we had to sleep side by side on hard, wooden floors without mattresses or any type of cushioning. To make matters worse, Uncle Arthur, Lorchen's father, was snoring so loudly that few of us could get a good night's sleep. If we awakened him, we might get a few minutes reprieve before he fell asleep again, snoring more loudly than ever.

For some time now, we had been without electricity and were solely relying on oil lamps and candles. Since both were in short supply, we used them sparingly and lit them only in emergencies. So, as soon as darkness set in, we had no choice but to retire for the night. It was an especially dreary existence for the young people having to go to bed at dusk every night, but we dared not complain for everyone was doing his or her best to get through these trying times.

The Dahms House

Chapter 16

On the eighth of May 1945, Russian soldiers started going berserk, shouting and firing their weapons wildly into the air, scaring us out of our wits. Supposedly, word had reached them that the war had ended and this was their way of celebrating. The celebration had tragic consequences though as three of their own men were killed. This unfortunate incident occurred as some of the soldiers attempted to cut down a tree using their automatic weapons to sever the trunk. Three of their comrades peeling potatoes behind a barn were struck by stray bullets and killed instantly.

We thanked God that the war finally had come to an end.

To supplement our meager diet, my mother did something very foolish one night. While everyone was asleep, she stole quietly out of the house and went next door, where the soldiers had settled in for the night. She slipped past the sentry and made her way into the cellar where their provisions were stored. With her bare hands, she scooped some lard from a large barrel into her apron. Then groping around in the dark room, trying to find the exit, she almost gave herself away by bumping into a barrel with a loud thud. After waiting a few anxious moments, she managed to slip past the drowsy sentry again, clutching her precious lard. She could easily have been killed as a shadowy figure stealing around in the dark and being out long after the imposed curfew. The lard, still wrapped in her apron, was well hidden in the barn. Once the soldiers left and we could return to our home, there would be potato pancakes. It was something to look forward to with great anticipation.

At the end of May, the soldiers were still with us. My blond, handsome dance partner occasionally showed up at our door, but I kept a discreet distance, not wishing to encourage him further.

The occupation was a hardship on us, but it may have been a blessing in disguise. As long as we lived under their protection, we were safe from marauding gangs of Russian soldiers looting and raping at will. The neighboring villages were not faring as well and were totally at their mercy. Last night, a group of drunken soldiers wreaked havoc in the next village. After hours of partying, they went looking for girls. Going from house to house, they came upon an eighty-five-year-old woman. Since she was bedridden and in ill health, she thought she had nothing to fear. When they could not find any girls, they decided that she would have to do. They promptly loaded her into a wheelbarrow and carted her off to their drunken orgy, where she was repeatedly assaulted throughout the night.

These were the times we lived in, never knowing what the next day would bring.

Chapter 17

The twenty-ninth of May 1945 was my sixteenth birthday. There were no presents or cake, not even a card. It was just another day with more milk and potatoes. Frau Voelkner, a woman in her thirties who was also staying at the Dahms house with her two young sons, offered to do my hair as a birthday gift. My long tresses were swept upward into a stylish hairdo held in place with hairpins and her precious pomade. She used it very sparingly since there would not be anymore once it was gone. I felt so very grown up with my new hairdo, but with no place to go to show it off.

By early afternoon, I did have a place to go. I, along with everyone else, was ordered to shovel manure for the rest of the day. The Russian commander thought the heaps of dung piled high next to the cow barns were offensive and wanted them removed immediately. So here I was on my sixteenth birthday, standing up to my ankles in cow manure and tossing pitchfork after pitchfork of this smelly mess onto horse-drawn wagons all afternoon long. By the end of the day, my new hairdo was in total disarray and I was a dirty, smelly mess myself. It was a birthday I knew I would never forget.

In the first week of June, there was a sudden burst of activity in the village. The soldiers were moving out, piling their trucks high with our furniture and household goods. They were carting off our belongings as we helplessly looked on. We learned that after weeks of inactivity, the troops were getting restless. Fearing for the women's safety, the commander was moving them deep into the forest. In a way, we were glad they were leaving, but leaving with them was the protection we had enjoyed these past few weeks.

As uncomfortable as it was at the Dahms house, we decided to stay. There was some safety in numbers and, besides, our home was in shambles with just the beds and a few odd pieces of furniture remaining.

CHAPTER 18

With the troops gone, disorganized bands of soldiers were an ever-present threat. At times, they were just passing through, but all too often they made themselves at home by drinking and raising a ruckus all night long. After sleeping off the effects of their drunken binge, they were on their way, soon to be replaced by others.

Late one afternoon, a large group of soldiers had been partying two houses down the street from us. As the evening progressed, their voices became louder and more boisterous until shortly before midnight their drunken brawl was totally out of control. They were shooting their weapons into the air and causing such a disturbance that no one at the Dahms house was able to sleep. Before long, they were pounding on our back door. We tried to ignore them and kept very quiet hoping that they would go away. But rifle butts were soon battering down the door, giving Lorchen, Ilse, and me just enough time to take refuge in a small storage room in the back of the house. To hide its entrance, a wardrobe was hurriedly pushed in front of it. I was still in my nightgown and shaking like a leaf from sheer fright. At sixteen, I had never dated, kissed, or even held hands with a boy. The thought of being raped repeatedly by a gang of drunken soldiers was almost more than I could bear. I thought death would be more merciful. I whispered to Ilse, "Should they find us, I do not want to be seen like this. I need a piece of clothing to pull over my nightgown."

It was her grandmother's house and she knew her way around this room even in the dark. Silently she handed me something from a pile of rags on the floor. Hurriedly I slipped what appeared to be a ragged knit shirt full of holes over my head and then wiped my hands across the wooden floor, hoping to gather enough dust to dirty my face. Should we be discovered, I wanted to look as ugly and unattractive as possible. All the while, the soldiers were rummaging through the house, turning everything upside down while looking for women. Suddenly, they were outside our tiny window. Shining a bright flashlight into the room, they discovered our little hideaway. Shouting with glee, they rushed back into the house and were soon at our door, pushing the wardrobe aside. Ilse and I took flight behind the door while Lorchen was desperately trying to scramble beneath the pile of discarded clothing on the floor. There were so few places to hide in this very small room.

As the door flung open, two soldiers with flashlights in hand and automatic rifles slung carelessly over their shoulders entered the room. It did not take them long to discover our hiding place. I never felt so helpless and frightened as they looked us over from head to toe. Not knowing what else to do, I stared cross-eyed back at them and then, grabbing my stomach, started wailing in a loud and mournful voice. Ilse, scared out of her wits, soon followed suit. Now we were both howling like wolves.

The soldiers stared at us in disbelief, took a step backward, and almost landed on top of Lorchen, who was still cowering under the pile of rags on the floor. Once discovered, they grabbed her harshly by the wrists and proceeded to drag her into the next room. Not a sound was coming from her lips, but her eyes were wide with terror and her face was ashen white. Ilse made a dash for an old wardrobe standing in the corner of the room. Once inside, she frantically tried to shut the door, but I was close behind her. I grasped the door with such force that it tore out of its hinges and crashed to the floor with a loud bang. As I slid into the wardrobe beside her, she hissed at me, "Look at what you have done. Why did you have to follow me? Now they are going to find both of us."

Her angry reaction took me completely by surprise. I guess that under duress we sometimes do and say things that are completely out of character. Soon several soldiers were back looking for us, stumbling around in a drunken stupor while still clutching their automatic weapons. I watched in horror as two of them pulled Ilse out of the wardrobe and dragged her into the next room.

Soon they were back and motioned for me to come out. When I did not respond to their command, a tug-of-war ensued, with them pulling with all their might and my resisting with every ounce of strength that I possessed. It soon became evident that my resistance was hopeless. One of the soldiers, reeking strongly of alcohol, became increasingly impatient and reached for his gun, thrusting it into my midriff section as if to fire. Instantly, I raised my hands in a sign of surrender. To my relief, he slowly lowered his weapon. Being intoxicated and angry, he would have pulled the trigger in a heartbeat without giving it a second thought. *Dear God, I am at my wit's end. What am I to do?*

Slowly I crawled out of the wardrobe, pretending to be crippled and unable to walk. The soldiers half dragged and half carried me into the adjoining room, where the floor was still littered with our bedding. It looked like doomsday had arrived. Some of the older women were weeping while others, with their heads bowed, were praying. Everyone looked so sad and distraught, having nurtured and looked after our needs for most of our lives; they were now standing by helplessly and could not protect us from one of the worst misfortunes that could befall a woman.

Uncle Arthur, his jaw set tight and a stoic expression on his face, stared straight ahead. He wanted to intercede but was helpless to do so. The only signs of his inner turmoil were his clinched fists and the flexing of his jaw muscles. A loving father but a strict disciplinarian, he rarely allowed his eighteen-year-old daughter to date. Now he had to look on as she was about to be dragged off and violated by a gang of rough, drunken soldiers. A man of few words and strong self-discipline, I hoped he would not lose his composure and do something foolish. Nothing would be accomplished, but he might lose his life in the process, leaving Lorchen an orphan. Her mother died of tuberculosis while she was still a small child.

The women were herded together into the middle of the room like slaves about to be sold to the highest bidder. The soldiers closely guarded the door leading to the entrance hall. My mother frantically pleaded with the officer in charge, clawing at his uniform and repeating over and over, "Please, do not take my daughter. She is but a little girl. If you must take someone, take me instead." He finally lost his patience, grabbed her harshly, and hurled her across the hall, where she landed with a sickening thud against the opposite wall.

My fear suddenly turned to anger, and I vowed right there on the spot that I would never, ever give in to these brutes. Escape was out of the question. Physically, I was not strong enough to take them on, so in desperation I decided to act like a completely deranged person. I would do such repulsive things that no one would want me. While still cowering on the floor, I started grunting like an animal with my tongue hanging out and saliva dripping out of both sides of my mouth. Cross-eyed and salivating, I stared wildly about the room, my arms aimlessly flailing through the air, at times pulling at my hair or pawing the person next to me. Even some of our elders took notice, staring at me in disbelief. They probably thought the poor girl had taken leave of her senses. The officer in charge was growing impatient and was ready to go. He walked toward us, stared at me in obvious disgust, and then gave me a swift kick with his boot, causing me to fall backward. After gathering the women and girls, he and his fellow soldiers disappeared with them into the night.

Drained of all energy, I lingered a few moments on the floor before I got up, ever so thankful for having been spared and still trying to comprehend what had just taken place. Apparently, my impromptu performance convinced them that I was truly deranged.

I checked on my mother to make sure she was all right. Her shoulder was a little sore, but otherwise she was fine. Quietly, we went back to our assigned places too numb to speak and fearing for our loved ones. As I walked past a mirror, I caught a glimpse of myself. My hair was disheveled and my face streaked with dirt. The piece of clothing I had so hastily put on looked like a man's long-sleeved, knit undershirt or what was left of it. One arm was partially ripped off while the other one was completely gone, and the entire garment was full of holes. Men usually wore these heavy, white undershirts on cold, wintry days beneath their regular clothing. This one had certainly seen better days. I curled up on the floor and wrapped myself in a blanket, but sleep would not come. So many thoughts continued to run through my mind as I lay there staring into the darkness. At times like these, the night seemed so long.

Suddenly, I detected the faint sounds of horses' hooves in the distance. Civilians never ventured out at this time of night, so this could only mean that soldiers were on the prowl again. We hoped that they were just passing through and were not overly concerned until we heard them dismount just outside our house. With the door already destroyed from our previous encounter, they walked right in, giving me barely enough time to leap into a large wardrobe bulging with suits, coats, and dresses. I squatted down in the farthest corner and wrapped both arms around my legs to pull them as close as possible to my body. On the bare, wooden floor, I soon heard heavy footsteps coming straight toward me. The wardrobe door swung open and a soldier started taking out piece after piece of clothing, inspecting everything closely by the light of an oil lamp. With each piece of clothing removed, he was coming closer. Paralyzed with fear, I shook uncontrollably while knowing full well what would be in store for me if I were discovered.

My eyes filled with tears as I lifted my face toward heaven and started to pray, asking God over and over again to see me safely through this terrible ordeal. Never had I prayed so hard and earnestly in my life. Since we did not have a church in our village, religion had never played a major role in our lives. We believed in God, celebrated the religious holidays, and always said our prayers at night, but we seldom attended church services. One Sunday each month a minister would visit our village and hold services in a parishioner's home. I always tried to attend. While sitting in the wardrobe, it seemed there was no one to turn to. God was my only hope.

Minutes seemed like hours as the soldier continued to rummage through the wardrobe. As he got closer and just a few more pieces of clothing separated us, to my utter amazement, the light began to flicker and suddenly there was total darkness. While the soldier was searching for another light, I leapt out of the wardrobe and into an adjoining room where my brother, Kurt, and his friend Horst had been sleeping under a thick, heavy featherbed. I took them totally by surprise as I slipped in between them. The boys, sensing the danger, immediately covered me from head to toe.

The soldier soon returned with a new light and continued to rifle through the wardrobe. I was ever so thankful to God for extinguishing the light in the nick of time, allowing me to escape. Coincidence? Perhaps, but I chose to believe otherwise.

As the soldiers were about to leave, one of them noticed the unusually big bulge under the featherbed and kicked the bedding, with his heavy boot striking my toes. After a few anxious moments, he moved on, and as quickly as they had appeared the soldiers vanished back into the night.

I was completely exhausted, physically and mentally. The phrase "being scared to death" took on a new meaning for me. I knew that I could not stay in this house one moment longer. I would sleep in the barn for the rest of the night.

As I left the house, I was shaking so hard that I could barely put one foot ahead of the other. Every part of my body and every tooth in my mouth was aching. Blood was trickling down my legs as I began menstruating two weeks ahead of time. The trauma of the last few hours had a devastating effect on body and mind. It seemed I had aged years in the span of a few hours. I slowly climbed up to the loft of the barn, hollowed out a place in the hay, and curled up in the fetal position. Gradually, the shaking subsided and I fell into a restless sleep.

The women returned in the early morning hours and no mention was ever made of the events of that terrible night.

We decided to move back into our house. It would be good to have some privacy again, and my mother was finally able to retrieve the hidden lard. With doors and windows closed to keep the aroma from drifting over to our neighbors' house, she prepared a large batch of potato pancakes for us. We ate to our hearts' content, not having tasted anything quite so good for some time.

We soon discovered that the soldiers had infested our house with fleas and lice. Every morning, there were little specks of blood on our bed linens where the fleas had feasted on us during the night. We washed the linens almost daily, but without insecticides or detergent it was a hopeless battle. At times, we itched so badly that our skin was scratched raw and bloody.

Lorchen Lutz

Chapter 19

Since all means of communication had long been disrupted, we were totally cut off from the rest of the world. There had been no word from my aunt in Berlin. We were fearful for her, as there had been months of constant heavy bombing from the air, followed by the Russian ground assault which was accompanied by relentless artillery fire. When she finally managed to get a letter through to us, we were so relieved that she was alive and well.

From her letter, we learned that, like everyone else, she had her share of frightening experiences and hardships. Shortly after the Russian assault on the city began, she witnessed her first tragedy. A neighbor living in an apartment building across the street foolishly ventured out to do one last errand during the heavy shelling. A small store nearby remained open in spite of the bombardment so that neighborhood customers could do some last-minute shopping for scarce food supplies. She thought she had made it safely home and was already at her apartment house door when a shell fragment struck her in the throat, severing a major artery. Help came too late. Within minutes, she died in a pool of blood.

On the same day, a neighbor's teenage daughter was running from her parents' butcher shop to their apartment across the street when she was hit in the calf by a piece of shrapnel, which left an ugly wound. She needed immediate medical attention. Her parents were physically unable to accompany her to the nearest doctor. Everyone else was too frightened to venture out and risk being seriously wounded or killed. The poor girl was obviously in distress, so my aunt volunteered to take her to a doctor a few blocks away. They ducked into doorways and crouched behind anything that would afford them a little protection from the continuous shelling. The doctor cleaned and bandaged the wound and then urged them to stay until there was a lull in the attack. But fearing that it would only get worse, they decided to make a run for it, wanting to be with family and friends during the harrowing ordeal. They were soon on their way again, running from doorway to doorway, until they finally made it home, frightened but unhurt.

My aunt and her neighbors then huddled in the cellar as the shelling continued, not knowing what the next day or even the next few hours held in store for them. Periodically, they would dash up to their apartment for some food and water to sustain them a little while longer.

After a few days, the city suddenly fell silent. The destruction and bloodshed were finally over. This once beautiful city, a center of culture and learning, lay in ruins, and its people were left to fend for themselves as best as they could.

Russian soldiers were soon swarming throughout the city, going in and out of houses and apartments, taking watches, jewelry, and anything else they desired. My aunt and her neighbors were not spared.

Soldiers barged in and out of the cellar, taking their valuables and food. The first time my aunt ventured upstairs to check on her ground-floor apartment, she was shocked to discover that the Russian soldiers were using her home as a stable for their horses. A bowl of sardines, which she had left on the kitchen table, had been thrown against the wall, leaving the little fish sticking to the painted surface. It certainly made for an odd sight. Instead of using the bathroom facilities, some of the soldiers left their calling cards in the kitchen, covering up the results of their crude behavior with bowls taken from her cupboard. She also found that there was no food left in her apartment. The soldiers had eaten every edible scrap.

She made a fast retreat back into the cellar, where she wondered how she was going to survive. Some of her neighbors came to her aid by offering to share what little food they had left. The apartments on the upper levels were not as badly ransacked as those on the ground floor, and they were able to salvage some of their food before the soldiers discovered it.

Since my aunt's apartment was uninhabitable, a neighbor lady living alone offered her a place to stay while the pillaging continued. Every door lock in the apartment building was smashed or otherwise disabled, affording the occupants little privacy or security as the soldiers walked in and out at will.

In some of the apartments, the toilets were stopped up when soldiers used the bowls to wash potatoes for their meals. In the process, they sometimes flushed them down the drain, probably never knowing that the toilet bowls were not intended for washing vegetables.

Once my aunt barely avoided being raped. While still living with Frau Werner, whose home she was sharing at the time, a soldier wandered into the apartment late one afternoon. To the women, both in their midforties, he looked young enough to be their son. With such a great age difference, the women thought they had nothing to fear. Instead of rifling through their belongings and looking for material things, he ordered both of them into the bedroom. Frau Werner became hysterical and began screaming at the top of her lungs. The soldier slapped her across the face in an attempt to quiet her. When she would not comply, he lunged instead at my aunt as she was trying to escape. He managed to grasp the scarf she was wearing around her neck. A tug-of-war ensued, with her pulling so hard that the scarf was ripped in half, causing the soldier to lose his balance and giving her a chance to make her escape. In the end, both women were spared. The soldier left the apartment, never to return.

She closed her letter by saying that she was back in her own home after several days spent cleaning and repairing the damage as best she could. She also said that the food shortage was acute in the city but for us not to worry because she was getting by. At last, we knew that she was alive and well. We hoped that we would be able to see each other in the near future.

West Berlin, Germany, 1945, after WWII ended.

CHAPTER 20

For the next few days, an officer went from house to house recruiting women to do laundry for his troops. There were mountains of underwear and uniforms piled high by the river's edge, having been worn by the soldiers for weeks on end and crawling with vermin of all kinds. The women scrubbed their hearts out, but without hot water and very little detergent, it was almost impossible to get the clothing clean. By the end of the day, their hands were rubbed raw. To make matters worse, the female soldiers were throwing back, time and again, the already washed clothing, making the women do them over again. The female soldiers seemed just as cruel as their male counterparts.

My mother was determined that I would not be subjected to washing their dirty clothes. By the time the officer showed up at our house, I was tucked into bed, my breathing was labored, and my face was bright red after giving it a brisk rub. He looked me over while my mother was trying to convince him that I was very ill. He probably did not understand a word she was saying, but he seemed satisfied and was soon on his way without uttering a single word. We were truly relieved that I would not have to wash their dirty rags, but for the next few days I would have to keep a low profile and stay indoors.

CHAPTER 21

Some families began to run out of food. Frau Jahn, a tall, stately woman in her thirties, walked past our house every morning with a basket over her arm and clutching a knife. Out in the meadow, she gathered grass and weeds for her daily pot of soup, which for the time being was her family's only nourishment. She was a refugee from one of the eastern provinces and had made it safely to our village with her two small children before the fast advancing Red Army arrived. She left most of her belongings and her treasured family heirlooms behind. Now she was assigned a small room in one of the farmhouses, which was a far cry from the beautiful home that once was hers. Her husband, a head forester by profession, was drafted into the German army and attained the rank of an officer before he was killed in action on the eastern front. Hers was but another life changed forever by this war. Despite the hardships, she endured. She bid everyone she met along the way with a cheery, "Good morning," as she made her daily trip to the meadow.

For many of us, it was a struggle just to survive. Our supply of table salt was gone, and we had to rely on dirty, red chunks of salt usually reserved for the livestock. When that was gone, we did without. It seemed that everything we had worked so hard for was taken from us.

Our farm animals were the next to go. Daily, large herds of cattle were passing through our village on their way to Russia. They were not milked at regular intervals, causing their udders to become so enlarged that every step was painful. If it was close to nightfall when they arrived in our area, the soldiers set up camp with the cattle on the outskirts of the village and erected wooden stalls for milking. This job always fell to the local women. Although I had never milked a cow before, I soon found myself in a small enclosure with one. She made it quite clear that she did not want any part of me. Well, the feeling was mutual. I did not want to be there either. Her udder was swollen and apparently painful to the touch. When I got close to her, she jumped and kicked, scaring me out of my wits. A soldier seeing my dilemma finally came to my aid and tied her up in such a way that it restricted her movements. I managed to extract enough milk from this poor creature to relieve some of her discomfort. It was usually long past midnight before the last cow was milked and we could go home. Since I was not used to this kind of work, the muscles in my hands stayed sore for days.

It was a real struggle for my mother to keep food on the table. As the soldiers drove another herd through the village, she managed to separate a cow from the herd right under their noses and lead her quickly into a barn. She was much braver than I could ever be. I guess that in her desperation she threw all caution to the wind and had no thought of the consequences. We were so thankful to have good, nourishing milk again.

As the cattle drive continued in full swing, the soldiers were rounding up young people from all of the surrounding villages to assist them. My brother, Kurt, and I were not spared. After being notified, we had to leave on short notice. Since we had to travel on foot and carry our belongings, we would have to travel light and take only the barest necessities.

It was late in the afternoon when we said our good-byes and were taken on a horse-drawn wagon to one of the neighboring villages. For lack of better accommodations, we would have to spend the night in a church located in the center of the village square. As the afternoon progressed, more and more young people arrived by truck and wagon.

I dreaded the thought of days filled with dust, dirt, constant milking, and long hours on the trail. Our evening meal consisted of a thick piece of black bread. With a blunt, dirty knife and hands that obviously had not been washed in days, a soldier half cut and half tore off large chunks of bread. We ate it slowly, savoring every bite. It was soggy and stuck to the roofs of our mouths and to our gums and teeth, but we did not mind. We dislodged it with our fingers and kept on eating. It was bread, and it tasted so good.

As night fell, the old church with its thick walls and tiny windows was cold and damp. Quietly, we found a place to settle down on one of the wooden benches. They were so hard and uncomfortable that I spent most of the night sitting up, all the while longing to be back in my warm, cozy bed.

The next morning, we were herded back onto trucks and wagons without food or water. As the vehicles lumbered down the cobblestone road, I took one last look at our village in the distance.

It was a short journey to one of the larger farms, where hundreds of cows were rounded up for the long cattle drive to Russia. A large kettle of soup was bubbling over an open fire, tended by female soldiers. Most of them looked like well-endowed peasant girls. We jokingly called them gun molls. They served us their greasy fare: a soup made of beef, a few vegetables, and water with large globs of fat floating on top. But we were not choosy. We were only too glad to have something to eat, fat and all.

One of the female soldiers was fascinated with the clear plastic spoon that I brought from home. Never having seen such an eating utensil, she walked over, handed me her metal one, and took the plastic one for herself.

Hilde, a girl from our village, fell ill with dysentery. I was not well acquainted with her. She was from the city and her parents, fearing for her safety during the bombing raids, sent her to live with relatives in the country. She was as thin as a reed, and her long, blonde hair was always styled in the latest fashion. Now she looked so frail and weak with her beautiful hair disheveled. Since no one seemed to be looking after her, I offered my help, which she gratefully accepted. Leaning heavily on me, we spent the next few hours trudging back and forth to the latrine.

By noon the soldiers were ready to start on the long cattle drive. The officer in charge decided that Hilde was too ill to travel and requested that I take her home. We said our good-byes and were soon on our way. We had to walk through meadows and fields, as using the roads was far too risky for two girls. For Hilde, it was a slow and difficult trip. She had to rest quite often to catch her breath. Whenever we spotted soldiers in the distance, we immediately dropped to the ground, staying there until they were out of sight. We still had a small river to cross, and since neither of us were good swimmers this presented a problem.

As we approached the river, we noticed, to our relief, that enemy troops must have placed a beam across it during the assault, since I had never seen one there before. The beam was far too narrow for both of us to go across. She would have to make it on her own. Volunteering to go first and carrying our belongings, I slowly ventured out onto the beam, expecting at any moment to plunge down into the river a few feet below. But all went well, and I arrived safely on the other side. Now it was Hilde's turn.

She stared at the water and then at me, her eyes silently pleading, *I really do not want to do this.* But there was no other choice; she would have to try. After a few shaky starts, she was finally on her way, slowly putting one trembling foot in front of the other while I shouted encouragement from the other side.

Several times she faltered but finally made it safely across. Totally exhausted, she took a short rest before we continued. As our village finally came into view, it was a comforting sight. Soon we would be home and safe at last. Our families would be happy to see us.

Once home, Hilde was promptly put to bed and my mother was overjoyed that I did not have to continue on the long, tiring cattle drive with the threat of rape ever present.

Over the past few weeks, most of our belongings were taken from us. I did not even have a pair of shoes to wear. My mother still had a pair of men's black, patent-leather shoes that were far too large for me, but it was better than going barefoot. The first time I wore them, a group of soldiers had a good laugh at my expense, pointing repeatedly at my feet. It made me so angry. First they stole our possessions, and then they found it amusing when we had to improvise and use the few things that were left to us.

I was beginning to lose track of time. I did not care anymore what time of the month or day of the week it was. I was just passing time with no hope for the future as one day blurred into another. We did not get any mail, and with no electricity, there was no radio or newspaper to keep us informed. We were totally cut off from the rest of the world.

Chapter 22

Last night, our village was terrorized by a group of drunken soldiers. They arrived late in the afternoon and picked our house at random, giving us barely enough time to escape to Anton's house. The drinking and carousing started immediately, their voices growing louder and more boisterous by the hour. We never could figure out where all their liquor came from; they seemed to have a never-ending supply of it.

After dark, they began looking for women. Many families had already retired for the night when they came knocking at their doors, breaking them down if there was not an immediate response. A mother of eight, sleeping next to her husband, was dragged out of bed and taken to our house, where she was assaulted by different soldiers throughout the night.

Emma, the girl who was so fearful of being impregnated as a result of a brutal rape, was also discovered hiding under a bed and promptly taken to their drunken orgy, resisting every step of the way. Hour after hour, she was assaulted. The last soldier was so intoxicated that he fell asleep while raping her. Too scared to move for fear of waking him and being assaulted again, she lay there motionless under his dead weight, barely able to breath, all the while enduring his foul breath. During her tortuous ordeal, she focused on the wall clock, watching it slowly tick the hours away until the first light of day when both of the women were finally released. Only partially clothed and shivering in the cool morning breeze, they fled to their homes, using the back way so no one would see them in their humiliating condition.

As soon as the soldiers arrived at our house, Margot, the daughter of neighbors, Lorchen, and I hid in the cellar located beneath a small bedroom in Anton's house. With the trapdoor closed and a heavy carpet placed over it, we cowered in total darkness. The cellar was stacked high with clothing and household goods, all hidden away from the enemy. We spent a very uncomfortable night. There was room for only one of us to lie down in those tight quarters. We finally resolved this dilemma by taking hourly turns throughout the night.

With the ruckus going on across the street, sleep was hard to come by anyway. For twelve long hours, we huddled there in total darkness and did not emerge until the last soldier was out of sight, ever so thankful that we were spared once more. Our ordeal paled when compared to what the other women had to endure. Emma had never dated or had any type of relationship with a man. Their nightmare was far from over. The days ahead would be filled with the anxiety of not knowing if they were pregnant or infected with a sexual disease. The sexual disease could be cured, but a child was a lifetime commitment.

Our house was in total disarray. The sickening, stale odor of cheap grain alcohol and the foul smell of their tobacco were wafting through the house, almost taking our breath away. The sheets would have to be washed and the bedding aired out. Everything would need a thorough cleaning before the home was livable again. The memory of what had happened here would not be as easily erased.

CHAPTER 23

After two weeks, my brother, Kurt, returned from the cattle drive a few pounds lighter and his shoes in tatters, but otherwise he was all right. Some of the others did not fare as well.

Anneliese and Edith, two very attractive young sisters from our village, had a hard time keeping the soldiers at bay. Before they left on the cattle drive, their mother took them aside and urged them never to give in and let the soldiers abuse and torture them. "Find a way to take your life," she said to them. "If you do not return, I will know that you are in a better and safer place where no harm will ever come to you again."

Several days into the cattle drive, they were about to be assaulted by a group of drunken soldiers. In desperation, Anneliese, the older of the two, jumped onto a horse-drawn wagon shouting, "If you want to rape us, you will have to kill us first." Then ripping open the top of her blouse and pointing a finger at her chest, she challenged them to shoot her right there on the spot. An older officer, hearing the commotion, walked over and promptly dispersed the tormentors with a few harsh commands. He was not a handsome man with his pockmarked face, but he was kind and compassionate. For the rest of the cattle drive, he took them under his wing and watched over them like a father. Perhaps somewhere faraway, a daughter anxiously was awaiting his return.

When they reached the recently established Polish border, officers of the Polish army would not permit them to enter the former German territory of eastern Pomerania. After a confrontation between them and their Russian counterparts, the herd of cattle was allowed to pass, but the Germans were persona non grata and not permitted to cross the border. Instead, they were assigned to work in a sugar beet factory. After a few days, they were released and each of them received a single loaf of bread for the long journey home. They slept in sheds and barns along the way, begging food from farmers after their meager supply of bread ran out. We were relieved and happy to have them back.

Chapter 24

By June 1945 our lives had come to a virtual standstill. The few shops in the neighboring village had not reopened. There was still no mail service. The trains were not running, and the electricity had yet to be restored. It seemed that we had stepped back in time with people fending for themselves as best as they could. When self-preservation is at stake, it brings out the best and the worst in people, revealing their true character. It is a lesson we would learn as something quite unsettling happened a few days later.

One of our own turned on us and sided with the enemy. He was a farmer living on the outskirts of the village. His home was always the first to be ransacked by roving gangs of soldiers. When one of them was about to assault his mentally and physically handicapped teenage daughter, it apparently was more than he could bear. He offered to drive the soldiers through the village, promising to find healthy girls for them if they would spare his daughter. The soldiers were only too glad to oblige, and they were soon on their way.

It was a strange-looking entourage that came racing through the village. The farmer was acting like a madman, bringing his whip down harshly on the horses' flanks. Standing up, a white butcher's apron tied around his middle, he kept pointing to different houses. The soldiers, sitting in the back of his wagon, were bouncing up and down, holding on for dear life and probably wondering what they had gotten themselves into.

We anxiously peered out from behind closed curtains, not knowing what to make of this spectacle. When we realized what was happening, all the girls went immediately into hiding. After a fruitless search, the soldiers had to be content with a couple of radios and a few household goods. As for the farmer, his conduct so angered the villagers that one of them turned him in to the Russian authorities for possession of a firearm, which was strictly illegal. The next day, he was picked up and never heard from again. It was a sad testimony to a people once living in peace and harmony but now turning on one another. These were the times we lived in, when self-preservation was foremost in everyone's mind.

After many weeks, our electricity was finally restored. It was such a relief not having to rely on smelly oil lamps anymore. And, for a change, we were able to enjoy the evening hours instead of having to retire as soon as darkness set in.

We also had bread at last. A bakery in the next village reopened, but we had to stand in long lines for just one loaf of bread. It was of poor quality, but we did not mind after having to do without it for so long. We enjoyed every bite.

CHAPTER 25

On July 7, 1945, we buried two little boys. With proper medical care and an adequate diet, both probably would have survived. Wernie, the eight-year-old, had fallen from a horse. Shortly thereafter, he complained of stomach pains and was rushed to a poorly equipped, makeshift medical facility some miles away. Lacking the necessary diagnostic tools, such as X-ray equipment, doctors examined him and dismissed his condition as merely a stomachache. He was sent home, where he died a few days later of a massive infection. Something must have ruptured internally as a result of the fall. The other little boy, barely a year old, died of malnutrition. His family was poor and had many mouths to feed. Had there been enough food to go around, his life also would have been spared.

Many businesses remained closed, including the carpentry shop in the next village where for generations our coffins had been made. Some of the villagers got together and fashioned two small boxes out of boards. The little coffins looked so pitifully plain that Wernie's father decided to paint them white. The paint was of poor quality and probably did not have time to dry. As a result, all of the black tuxedoes worn by the pallbearers were smudged with white paint while carrying the crudely constructed caskets to the grave.

Wernie's family managed to scrape together a little food and drink for the gathering that followed at their home. This was a far cry from the funerals of the past. Whenever someone in the village had passed away, the body was bathed and prepared for burial by one of the local women. The open casket was on display in the best room of the house, where all mirrors were draped in black cloth as a sign of mourning. On the day of the funeral, the pastor conducted a short service after which family and friends gathered around the coffin one last time to say their farewells. A black hearse, adorned with black-fringed valances, carried the deceased on his last journey to the cemetery. It was drawn by horses draped in heavy, black, formfitting blankets with openings only for the eyes, ears, and tails. These ensembles were especially made and designed for funerals. Behind the hearse walked the pallbearers dressed in black tuxedoes and stovepipe hats. They were followed by a brass band of six or eight musicians playing some of the saddest funeral music. Next came the family walking or riding in a horse-drawn buggy, and they were followed by friends and relatives in carriages or on foot. Everyone dressed entirely in black.

The procession was always such a sad and depressing sight. Upon arrival at the cemetery, another short service was held at the gravesite, committing the soul of the departed into the hands of the Lord. After the funeral, family and friends gathered at the home of the deceased for a celebration. Tables, laid out with the best linen, china, and silver, were laden with food and drink. At times, these gatherings almost took on a party-like atmosphere where everyone all but danced.

CHAPTER 26

By mid-July the wild blueberries were once again ripening in the forest. In years past, it had always been such fun going blueberry picking. We usually went in groups, chatting and laughing all day long. This year it would be a different story. We contemplated whether we, a group of young girls, including my cousin Lorchen and her two friends Helma and Ilse should risk spending hours alone in the forest. But the thought of fresh fruit was so tempting that we threw all caution to the wind and decided to go anyway. With baskets in hand, we left early the next morning for the long walk to the forest. It was such a peaceful and quiet place. With soft, swishing sounds, the tall pine trees were gently swaying in the morning breeze while the birds were serenading us with their songs. These were the sounds of the forest: so soothing and comforting, a good remedy for our frayed nerves.

Although somewhat uneasy and constantly on the lookout for soldiers, we enjoyed a wonderful day. We ate our lunch and more than our share of blueberries. When it was time to leave in late afternoon, our baskets were not filled but our hearts were somewhat lighter. It had been a good day, and my mother would welcome the blueberries, which she would use to supplement our meager diet.

As we walked home from the forest, my throat began to ache. Thinking it was probably the result of laughing and talking too much, I was not concerned in the least. But as dinner approached, I did not feel like eating and went straight to bed. All throughout the night, my symptoms continued to worsen, and by morning my throat was so sore that I was barely able to swallow. My mother was quite concerned. A number of people had fallen ill lately with diphtheria and typhoid fever. It had reached epidemic proportions throughout the country.

Our physician in the next village had not resumed his practice at the time. We had to travel some distance to see another doctor. Herr Bassow, one of our neighbors, was kind enough to take my mother and me there in his horse-drawn wagon. It was a bumpy ride on narrow, cobblestone roads with me bundled up in blankets and lying on a soft featherbed in the back of the wagon.

The doctor's office was crowded with standing room only. We registered and went back outside to patiently await our turn. I had a high fever and was dozing on my makeshift bed when we were finally called back into the doctor's office. He took one look at my throat and announced solemnly, "Diphtheria. We will have to quarantine her immediately." With an anxious look on her face, my mother asked, "What are her chances, Doctor?" Checking my throat once more, he shook his head and said, "Only God knows. I have nothing to treat her with. All I can do is make her as comfortable as possible and hope for the best."

I was soon admitted to the makeshift hospital next door, and my mother was on her way home after a tearful good-bye. A large, two-story home was temporarily converted into a hospital to house and care for the many people who had fallen ill with these terrible, life-threatening diseases. The ground floor housed the diphtheria patients while the typhoid patients occupied the top floor. The hospital staff was made up of volunteers with only a few nurses available. Everyone was working long hours without pay or any other type of compensation, putting their lives and those of their loved ones at great risk, for both diseases could be deadly. It was truly a labor of love and compassion for their fellow man.

I was assigned to a room already crowded with patients of all ages. The beds were pushed so close together that there was barely enough room to walk. We had to furnish our own toiletries, towels, and sheets. Not knowing that I would be detained, I had brought none of these items and had to make do without until my mother returned.

There was no one to supply the hospital with food. The volunteers went from door to door and begged for a few crusts of bread or whatever other food people could spare. My throat was so sore that my breathing was labored. I knew that I would have to eat to survive, but trying to swallow the hard crusts of bread or whatever other food was available was pure torture. No matter how long I chewed this food, it still scratched my throat, bringing tears to my eyes every time I swallowed. At times, I would rather not have eaten at all. How good it would have been to have some soft food for a change, but I did not complain. These were harsh times, and we were very thankful to have anything to eat at all.

As the days went by, my high fever gradually subsided. The soreness in my throat and my breathing difficulties were also improving, so the doctor finally allowed me to get out of bed under strict orders not to exert myself. A few days later, he caught me in the kitchen drying dishes and gave me a harsh tongue-lashing with the warning that he would promptly send me back to bed if I did not follow his orders. I was truly sorry to have him angry with me, but in all fairness I did not consider drying dishes physical exertion. I was just trying to lend a helping hand to the overworked staff.

Dr. Appel, a tall, broad-shouldered man probably in his early fifties, was a kind but no-nonsense person. His face was pleasant but not what I would consider handsome. One of his arms was slightly withered, an affliction he was born with. The only doctor available for miles around, he worked almost nonstop with his beautiful, blonde nurse by his side, caring for the sick and dying without many of the necessary supplies and almost no medication available.

The staff had to divide their time between the two floors, which probably added to the threat of spreading the diseases even further. For me, the days went by ever so slowly as I idled the time away visiting with other patients and sitting for hours looking out the window. I was anxious for the day when I could go home.

Dr. Appel finally signed the discharge papers with a stern warning that I must not engage in any strenuous activities until my next appointment. He did not need to worry. Once home, instead of feeling better each day I felt worse. I had no pep or energy. I spent my days resting and unable to get out of bed. When I started to experience chills, fever, constant headaches, and general achiness, I was bundled up again and taken back to Dr. Appel. The diagnosis this time was typhoid, the dreaded disease that had taken so many lives. I was not even allowed to say good-bye to my mother. I was immediately admitted to the second floor that housed the typhoid patients. The room was large with every available space taken up by beds. Again, there was barely enough room for the doctor and nurses to squeeze through. Every bed was occupied except for a baby's bed. The little one had just been discharged. The bed assigned to me was next to a window. At least I had plenty of fresh air.

The adjoining room was converted into a little chapel. Quite often, we heard murmured prayers for the ones who had lost their battle with this disease and were now on their journey to a better and safer place.

Each morning I received an injection as Dr. Appel and his nurse made their rounds. Food was so scarce that our one and only daily meal consisted of a bowl of thin, watery soup. Later in the afternoon, we were served a cup of unsweetened tea. It was barely enough to sustain life, but we knew that the medical professionals and volunteers were doing their best.

As soon as a patient went home or died, the bed was taken up by someone else. One day a young woman named Gretchen was admitted. Dark haired and quite pretty, she was desperate to get well so she could return home to her two small daughters. She also had been anxiously awaiting her husband's return from the war. The possibility that he was taken prisoner or even killed in battle never crossed her mind. She was so sure that he would return home someday.

My condition was not improving. I was growing weaker with each passing day. Usually by early afternoon, my temperature started to rise. By nighttime, it was so dangerously high that my body had to be repeatedly wrapped in wet, cold linens in an effort to bring the fever down to a safer level. At bedtime, I was afraid to close my eyes for fear of never waking up again. I asked Erika, a pretty, young nurse, to sit by my side and hold my hand until I drifted off to sleep. It was a restless sleep with the fever at times so high that I was delirious. This caused me to rise up in bed and, on a number of occasions, attack dear, sweet Erika. In the morning, when my temperature was almost back to normal and I was in my right mind, Erika would laugh about it and show me the scratch marks that I had inflicted on her.

Today, there were prayers again in the adjoining room. Hans has passed away. He was a young soldier who made it safely through the war but came home and died of typhoid fever. Ever since he was admitted, he had brightened our lives by telling funny jokes and stories to make us laugh. We would sorely miss him.

My condition was steadily worsening. My hair was beginning to fall out, and I continued to lose weight. I was no longer able to get out of bed. With death all around me, I had finally come to terms with the fact that I myself might die. I was not afraid anymore and faced each day with an almost apathetic and lethargic sort of calm. The future looked so bleak and seemed to hold little promise.

Gretchen had also taken a turn for the worse and was delirious for the last few nights. She began staring wildly about the room, jumping out of bed, and repeatedly climbing over the high railing of the baby crib. She pretended to be a baby herself, curling up in a fetal position and sucking her thumb. At dusk, she finally settled down, her breathing became labored, and she was no longer able to control her bodily functions. With a loud noise, her insides seemed to explode, spilling her body fluids onto her bedding and staining the white sheets a reddish brown. Soon, a terrible, nauseating stench filled the room. Gretchen was dying, and there was not a nurse in sight. Too weak to get out of bed, I managed to pull myself up to the open window and yell with all my might, hoping to alert someone downstairs. Soon, several nurses were at her side, each one grabbing a corner of her sheet and rushing her out of the room. Shortly thereafter, we heard the murmur of prayers in the little chapel and knew that Gretchen was gone, never to see her little ones or her beloved husband again. Her death left all of us shaken and wondering who was going to be next.

My mother made the long journey to the hospital quite often. She was not allowed to enter my room. She stood at the door and we communicated across the room. Today, she was visiting again but was not allowed to see me. She was beside herself, thinking that my end was near. She tried to make her way toward my bed but was restrained by several nurses and forcefully taken out of the room. She stood outside the building and stared up at my window while crying. I had to make it to the window to let her know that I was still alive. Two nurses lifted and propped me up so that I could wave to her from above. She looked so distraught but managed a weak smile and waved back.

Time seemed to stand still. I became listless and detached. I felt like I was a mere spectator watching life from the sidelines, not a participant anymore.

Many nights, the faithful nurse Erika still sat at my bedside, holding my hand and soothing my burning body with cold compresses. At times, she had to restrain me when I was thrashing about, my arms flailing aimlessly through the air. My arms and legs by now were very thin, and my long, blonde hair was all but gone.

One night I was especially restless, and sleep would not come as moonlight spilled through the open window and into the darkened room. There was something magical about a moonlit night. As a small child, I would try to count the stars and the different constellations. Now I had one last wish. I wanted to see the moon and a beautiful, starlit sky just once more. Although very weak, I slowly inched toward the window while the other patients were sleeping soundly. As I looked up at the dark endless sky and the glittering stars, with the full moon casting a soft, magical glow over the world around me, I was suddenly filled with an overwhelming desire to live. With tears trickling down my cheeks, I looked toward the heavens while a silent prayer was on my lips: *Please, dear God, make me well so that I may live. I do not wish to die.*

I lingered at the window, wishing to hold on to this special moment for a while longer. When I fell exhausted back onto my pillow, I felt somewhat assured that all was going to be well. No matter what hardships lay ahead, life was still worth living. For the first time in weeks, I fell into a sound sleep.

When I announced to a startled Dr. Appel the next morning that I was not about to die, that I was going to live, his face lit up. With a big grin, he assured me that he had done his best to keep me alive, but that the will to live and one's mental outlook played an important role in getting well.

I was now determined to get out of bed and get on with life, but the recovery process was ever so slow. After weeks in bed and very little nourishment, my legs were wobbly and my head was spinning as I took my first steps. But supported by nurses, I walked a little farther each day. I pleaded with Dr. Appel to allow me to go home, assuring him that I would strictly follow his orders, but the answer was always a big, "No!"

After several weeks, the day of my discharge finally arrived. As I said my good-byes, there were tears all around. I had nothing to offer them for their loving care but my heartfelt thanks and gratitude.

On the ride home, I noticed the landscape had changed. The first colors of autumn were visible. The harvest had begun and some of the fields were barren with only the stubble remaining. After being confined for weeks, I enjoyed the sights and sounds of the outside world once again. Even the smell of the horses pulling the wagon behind them and finally carrying me home was welcome. It was good to be back with family and friends.

I began to grow stronger with each passing day. Even my hair started to grow out. I was still confined to the house when one evening I heard the sound of music drifting through an open window into my room. Across the street, Anton was sitting on the front steps of his house, where he played a peppy tune on his accordion. He was soon surrounded by some of the young people of the village, all swaying and dancing to the rhythm of his music. I threw all caution to the wind, hurriedly slipped on a pair of shoes, and joined the merriment. I was keeping in time with the music and having the time of my life when my mother suddenly appeared. She was not at all amused. In fact, she was very angry with me for disobeying the doctor's orders. On the way home, I got a good tongue-lashing, but it was worth it. The music was so inviting. It made me feel so alive once again.

Ducherow, Germany. Apartment building used as a makeshift hospital in 1945 when epidemics of typhoid and diphtheria broke out. Top floor housed typhoid patients, bottom floor the diphtheria patients.

Chapter 27

All throughout the village, the threshing machines were humming once more as they harvested the grain from the fields. It had been planted in the spring by farmers whose age kept them from serving in the military, but now they would have to share the harvest with the occupational forces. In the years before the war, after the harvest there was always a large thanksgiving celebration. I remembered wearing a dirndl to these festivities. The gathered skirt was made of a colorful material; the blouse was white and beautifully trimmed with lace. A black vest, laced together up front, completed the outfit. On my head, I wore a wreath that my mother had made out of fresh flowers.

The festivities began with a parade through the village. The band was always first in line, followed by horse-drawn wagons, each of them decorated with fall flowers, fruits, and vegetables. The first wagon carried the harvest crown, which was woven out of straw and raised on a pole high above the wagon. Well-endowed farmers' wives, dressed in their Sunday finest, rode in the wagons while the rest of us brought up the rear.

After the procession made its way through the village, everyone gathered at the festival site. People from the neighboring villages often came and joined in the fun. There were games of chance and booths with a variety of items from trinkets to food and beverages. I loved to watch from the sidelines as the usually solemn farmers loosened up a little and twirled their ladyloves around on the dance floor.

It was hard for me to sit still whenever I heard music. I loved to dance and soon joined some of the older children on the dance floor. It was such fun to sway to our hearts content to the rhythm of the music. When evening came and it was time for me to go home, I always begged to stay a little longer. I could not wait to grow up.

The celebration often lasted far into the night with some of the revelers nursing a hangover the next morning, but the day filled with fun and laughter would linger on in our memories for years to come.

In the next village, there was a large horse training operation formerly managed by the German military. It had been there for years and the many acres of adjoining land were used for the production of feed. Some of the finest horses in the land were raised there for use by the German cavalry. The grain from these fields had not yet been harvested. To supplement our meager food supply, we set out night after night, with burlap bags and scissors, to do our own harvesting. After everyone had long retired, we would sneak out of the village, single file, in groups of five to ten, like common thieves. Once we reached the fields, we grabbed handfuls of wheat or rye, cutting off the upper portions of the plants, which held the precious grains. Hastily, we filled our bags and slipped quietly back into the village before daylight. Some of the fields were guarded throughout the night. On more than one occasion, we had to run for our lives when pursued by guard dogs, forcing us to leave some of our partially filled bags behind, but it did not deter us from returning for more. Since these fields formerly belonged to the German government, we had no qualms about taking this grain, which would have undoubtedly fallen into the hands of the occupying forces.

After the drying process, we separated the grain from the chaff by pounding the filled burlap bags repeatedly with wooden paddles. It was not the most efficient way to harvest the kernels, but it was the only one available to us. Periodically, we took a few pounds to the mill to have it ground into flour. Since we were not supposed to be in possession of any type of grain, the Russians were keeping a close eye on the mill. Whenever I saw their black staff car, I made a fast retreat and tried again another day. It would be good to have flour for baking over the long winter months ahead.

Some of the finest horses were trained here for use in the German Calvary

CHAPTER 28

The trees were beginning to shed their leaves and the days were getting cooler. It was time to put a few logs on the fire to take the chill out of the air. The wild geese were heading south to escape the harsh northern winter. Their noisy chatter could be heard for miles, as they were winging their way across the autumn sky. It signaled a passage of time. Another season gone by.

A command post (Kommandantura) had been established by the Soviet military in the next village. Many of our men, mostly farmers, were brought in for questioning. The interrogation was intense and usually lasted into the early morning hours. From our little village alone, six men did not return from these interrogations. We heard that some of them had been picked up by the notorious Russian secret police, known as the NKVD, for further questioning. During the war, several Russian soldiers escaped from a German prisoner of war camp and were observed wandering through a farmer's field. Suspecting that they were escaped prisoners, the farmers notified the German authorities.

Now the tables were turned and the farmers were questioned about their part in the capture of the Russian soldiers. They were brought before a military tribunal to be tried and sentenced. I shuddered to think of what fate would await them at the hands of this ruthless agency. It was most unlikely that their families would ever see them again.

Herr Lutz, our former mayor and another man from our village were sent to an internment camp at Neu Brandenburg, a town some distance from our area. Their offense was membership in the Nazi Party. Their confinement was strictly incommunicado; no contact of any kind with family or friends was permitted.

At considerable risk, relatives made the difficult journey to the camp in hopes of visiting the men. The relatives were not permitted to enter the compound or even to inquire as to their welfare. They were only able to view the prisoners from a distance through the high, wire fence surrounding the camp but were not able to positively identify their loved ones. They were shocked at the emaciated condition of all of the prisoners who appeared near starvation and would probably die of malnutrition or one of the many diseases that spread rampantly through these camps.

I guess starvation did not just take its toll on the body; it most likely had devastating effects on the mind as well. Our former mayor, who was one of the first ones to be picked up, was subjected to such hardships that he became disoriented and began to act in an irrational manner. He imagined himself to be someone in authority. He would ramble on and try to hold speeches despite beatings from the guards. He was finally put in solitary confinement, where death for him was a welcome relief after months of suffering untold atrocities at the hands of the guards. He died at the age of forty-four, still in the prime of his life. His family was never notified of his death or the disposition of his body.

It seemed the effects of this war would be with us for a long time to come, and they continued to claim lives.

Herr Herman Lutz
Mayor of Sprengersfelde, Germany, during WWII

CHAPTER 29

While still under Soviet occupation, we now had a new mayor in our village. She was a refugee from one of the eastern provinces who had not lived among us for very long. Frau Tina Stelzig, a woman in her fifties, unwittingly became the butt of jokes among the young men of the village. Her large, well-rounded breasts were situated somewhat higher than usual for a woman her age and looked totally out of proportion to the rest of her body. They jokingly dared one another to "accidentally" brush against her and lightly prick her breast with a straight pin to find out, once and for all, if they were real or just inflated balloons. These discussions were always followed by a round of raucous laughter. They acted so childish at times. But, of course, they never carried out their threat.

Frau Stelzig had some experience in the theater and suggested that we put on a play to liven up our dull existence a little. I had completely recovered from my illness and was eager to participate. We rented the dance hall in the next village and rehearsed for weeks.

When the big evening finally arrived, I could not eat a bite before the performance. To make matters worse, I was in a group of four girls who were going to be first on stage. We were dressed in white and each carried a colorful flower garland. As the music started, we danced across the stage to the strains of a beautiful Viennese waltz and got a good round of applause as we took our bows. The play did not get off to a good start though. One of the actors, who was playing the role of a waiter, was so nervous that he stumbled as he made his entrance and spilled food all over the stage. The potato dumplings, a slimy concoction cooked in milk, were rolling in all directions, causing some of the other so-called *actors* to slip and slide all over the place. One of them lost his balance altogether and landed flat on his back. Frau Stelzig, directing the play from the wings, almost had a heart attack. The audience thought it was hilarious and roared with laughter, thinking that it was all part of the play.

A dance was planned after the performance as we tried to put our worries aside for a little while and recapture, even for a few hours, some of the fun and gaiety of the past.

The large dance floor was surrounded by tables and chairs with the elderly sitting along the wall and watching the younger generation dance the evening away, at times even joining them for a dance or two. Young men from all of the surrounding villages usually gathered in groups while the young ladies, always dressed in their finest, sat prim and proper at tables where they sipped cold drinks or, if they were a little more daring, even a liqueur. As soon as the music started, the young men came dashing across the room to ask the girls to dance, with the older generation probably reminiscing about the time when they were young and gay and waltzing around this very room in the arms of their favorite girl or boy.

After the play, the four of us, still wearing our white dresses, were asked by Herr Landers, an elderly gentleman from our village, to join him at his table for a glass of liqueur. He enjoyed our dance and, in appreciation, wanted to buy us a drink. We did not care for alcoholic beverages and would have preferred to join the merriment on the dance floor, but it would have been so impolite and disrespectful to refuse his kind offer. Drinking at social events was a perfectly acceptable practice, even at our age. So there we were drinking liqueur on empty stomachs, ingesting something we did not even care for, just to please a kindly old gentleman who mistakenly thought this was a special treat for us. We held our breath as we downed the first one. This soon was followed by a second round of drinks and, before we finally said our thank-you, each of us had downed three glasses of liqueur on an empty stomach.

As we walked toward the dance floor, I whispered to Erika, "My head is spinning. I'm not feeling well." White as a sheet, she replied, "Neither am I." With that, she stumbled in the direction of the restroom. Sonya, who was walking ahead of us, was asked to dance by one of the young men. Usually an excellent dancer, she was trying to keep in step with the music. As her partner swung her around with a flourish, they both lost their balance and fell flat onto the dance floor. Helga and I made a fast exit before we also made spectacles of ourselves. We decided it was time to go home. The proprietor's son insisted on accompanying us to make sure we did not stumble into the creek that separated our two villages.

The next day, we all nourished hangovers and vowed never to take another drink again, no matter who did the asking.

Thus ended the evening we had looked forward to with much anticipation for quite some time.

CHAPTER 30

My brother, Kurt, gave up all hope of furthering his education. Under the present circumstances, there was no way we could send him to an institute of higher learning. He had such an inquisitive mind and as a boy would spend hours taking things apart to see how they worked, much to my mother's consternation. We lost a few watches in the process when he was unable to reassemble them again. For now, he would have to walk daily to the next village to start work in a carriage shop as an apprentice, building and repairing horse-drawn wagons. He was quite disappointed, but there were no other alternatives at this time.

A young Russian soldier named Boris was also recently assigned to the same village. He was in charge of the mail delivery for the troops stationed in this area and made his rounds in a horse-drawn carriage. He looked to be in his early twenties and had a dark complexion with somewhat handsome but definite Slavic features. He was a daily visitor at the carriage shop, making small talk and watching the men at work. When he learned that Kurt played the accordion, he extended an invitation to the youth of both villages for an evening of music and dancing at his place in the next village. We accepted his invitation somewhat reluctantly, not knowing what to expect, but the evening went well. He even shared his ration of salt herring and sausage with us. Kurt played the accordion while Boris looked on in amusement, at times joining in the fun. The language barrier was not much of a problem since all of us had acquired a few basic words in each other's language. The rest was accomplished with gestures and sign language. For the youth of both villages, this became a place where they could gather several nights a week.

Occasionally, Russian soldiers still came out at night to rob and plunder. But now we had Boris to protect us. He handed a few of his new German friends loaded guns and pistols. Then all of them jumped into his carriage and headed in the direction of the robbery, shooting their weapons into the air and causing such a ruckus that the soldiers usually took flight. Afterward, the weapons were always returned to him, as Germans were not allowed to possess any firearms.

Some nights we piled into his carriage for a ride through the countryside, with him always asking us to sing. We usually had to repeat his favorite song, "Marianka," a number of times before the evening was over and he deposited us back at our front door, where we told him good-bye in his native tongue. As unlikely as it seemed, once our enemy, he had become our friend.

Kurt Vetter

CHAPTER 31

Winter arrived and the days of November were beginning to be quite cold. To save on heat, we once again lived and slept in one room of the house. Our food situation did not improve. Our main staples were still potatoes, bread, and milk. We were all getting very tired of this limited diet. Day in and day out, our main meal consisted of potato dumplings cooked in milk. We were still using the dirty red salt normally reserved for the livestock. It made the food we cooked look very unappetizing but added a little flavoring to an otherwise bland diet. We were fortunate since some of our neighbors had been out of any kind of seasoning for weeks.

Late one night, a neighbor came rushing over and asked for my mother's help. Her husband had arrived after dark with a large ram in tow. No one asked any questions as to where it came from. After hurriedly butchering the animal, they worked feverishly throughout the night dissecting and packaging the different cuts of meat. My mother received her fair share of it, and for the first time in months, we had a little meat.

The very next Sunday, as the aroma of the roasting lamb filled our house, we could hardly wait until dinnertime. The meat had the strong taste of mutton, but to us it was a feast. It was the best meal we had eaten in a long time.

December arrived and Christmas was fast approaching. It would be our first under Soviet occupation and only a very simple celebration. The Soviets were communists and did not recognize Christmas as a holiday. However, they did not interfere with our religious activities.

Oh, how I longed for the Christmases of the past. A few days before the holidays, we would take a hatchet or saw and walk through the forest to find just the perfect tree, and then we baked cookies and wrapped gifts. We never decorated the tree until the day of Christmas Eve, adorning it with beautiful glass ornaments from years past and real wax candles. As children, we could hardly wait for the festivities to begin. When Santa finally arrived on Christmas Eve, we were full of anticipation and perhaps a little apprehensive for he always brought along a switch and would ask if we had been good little girls and boys. Of course, we always answered with a loud, affirmative yes. German children always had to recite a special little poem for Santa before he handed out our gifts along with cookies, candies, and always a delicious orange from Spain. After Santa's visit, we gathered around the tree, lit the candles, and sang Christmas carols. The next day, we enjoyed a feast of roast goose, potatoes, and a variety of vegetables. In the afternoon, relatives would come to visit for coffee and to sample the baked goods.

This year, our little tree was decorated with a few homemade ornaments. Most of our household goods, including our Christmas decorations, disappeared during the early days of the occupation. We did have flour to bake cookies though, but since we lacked some of the other ingredients, they were not very tasty.

On Christmas Eve, we lit a few candles, sang carols, and exchanged simple handmade gifts. This year there would not be a goose, the traditional meal on Christmas day. Instead, we would eat the last piece of mutton, which we had saved for this special occasion.

And so the year 1945 at last came to an end. It had been a year of unparalleled tragedy and turmoil for us: the defeat and occupation of our homeland by foreign troops; our lives exposed to cruel and ruthless victors; enduring a desperate shortage of food; and exposure to the dreaded diseases typhoid fever and diphtheria, which took a heavy toll of lives. But somehow we survived, and for this we were so grateful. Life in the past had been very difficult and we surely did not see much promise for the immediate future, but we at least had some hope for improvement of our day-to-day existence, for the food supply was gradually improving.

Several times a week soldiers on horseback came to our village trying to exchange food and various household items for vodka or any kind of alcohol. One of them dared me to ride his spirited horse. It looked more like a large pony with long, shaggy hair. As a reward, he offered me a small sack of grain. I foolishly accepted, but as soon as I was in the saddle, I knew that I had made a big mistake. The horse took off like a streak of lightning and raced through the village with me holding on for dear life. There was no way of stopping it as we headed out toward the open road. Pulling on its reins did not help, nor did it respond to any of my commands. As soon as the next village with its cobblestone streets came into sight, I decided to jump off. The impact of the fall would be far less severe on the dirt road than on the hard stones. Besides, I preferred not to have an audience. I eased over to the left side of the saddle and then dropped with a thud to the ground, while the riderless horse raced on with its reins flapping in the wind.

Other than a few scrapes and bruises, I was in one piece. When I arrived back at the village on foot, the soldiers had a good laugh at my expense but were not at all amused by the loss of their horse. I did get my hard-earned sack of grain though.

Chapter 32

January turned into February and the nights were extremely cold. To save on heat, we usually went to bed early. It was a good feeling to snuggle under a nice, warm featherbed while the cold north winds were howling around the eaves of the house outside. Occasionally, a neighbor came over to play checkers or cards, a welcome diversion on the long cold winter evenings.

Tonight, there was a full moon. Everyone had already retired for the night, but I was restless and could not sleep. In the darkened room, I lingered at the window for a long time, thinking of the future and hoping that soon there would be a better tomorrow for all of us. The hour was late when I finally slipped into bed and dropped off to sleep. A short time later, we were awakened by a loud knock on the door. Wondering who would call at this time of night, my mother hastily dressed and opened the door. We heard voices, and soon several soldiers entered the room as my brother and I peered sleepily out from underneath our warm covers. They glanced about the room and then motioned for me to get up and accompany them. I wondered, *Am I being taken in for questioning?* I certainly had not committed a crime, nor had I done anything that would make them come after me, especially at this time of night. Then it occurred to me that my house was probably not picked at random. I must have been spotted by the soldiers during one of their excursions to the village to buy vodka and they decided to pay me a visit.

Hurriedly, I threw on some warm clothes. My mother did not understand the Russian language and, as fearful as she was for my well-being, she dared not challenge their demands as they were the authority and could do as they wished.

As I stepped out the door, a blast of frigid air greeted me. It was a clear, frosty night with the freshly fallen snow glistening like diamonds in the moonlight, transforming the landscape into a beautiful winter wonderland. As we walked toward the waiting car, the only sound on this cold, still night was the crunching of our footsteps in the snow.

A soldier was sitting behind the wheel of a vintage-looking automobile, most likely an old German army staff car with some of its windows missing. As we drove away and the car picked up speed, a stream of frigid air was pouring in through the open windows, making it so unbearably cold that my teeth were chattering and my whole body was shaking uncontrollably. We passed through some of the neighboring villages and then headed through the forest on a long stretch of a narrow road toward the county seat.

As we reached the outskirts of town, the car came abruptly to a stop in front of a pub, which had already closed for the night. After repeatedly pounding on the door, the proprietor appeared at an upstairs window. The soldiers gestured for him to come down and open the door. With a robe hurriedly thrown over his pajamas, he rushed downstairs and unlocked the door.

We stepped into a cold, unheated room where the fire in the hearth had been extinguished hours before. Now everything suddenly became clear to me. They had made me come along for a night of drinking and carousing. So far, their behavior had been tolerable, but the thought of what might happen once alcohol clouded their minds was frightening.

As the officers took their seats around the table, they motioned for me to come over and join them. Instead, in direct defiance of their order, I slumped into a chair at a respectable distance, all the while staring at the floor. The proprietor served them drinks and then tried to hand one to me, but I refused by shaking my head. He then gently lifted my head and, looking me straight in the face, asked in a hushed tone, "Child, what are you doing here at this time of night and in this kind of company?" I did not bother to answer. Could he not see that I was not here of my own free will?

They ordered a second round of drinks and soon a heated discussion ensued. From their gestures and lively conversation, I gathered that they were not happy with my sullen and uncooperative behavior. They finally summoned the driver and asked him to take me home. As I slowly got up, still shaking like a leaf, one of the officers removed his heavy winter coat and draped it over my shoulders. I told him, "Thank you," in his native tongue, speaking for the first time since leaving home.

As we headed for the car, the driver motioned for me to sit up front with him, where it was not quite as drafty as in the backseat. Silently we drove through the forest. The branches of the tall evergreen trees, laden with snow, looked so beautiful in the moonlight. I was starting to relax. Soon, I thought, I would be home and back in my nice, warm bed.

As we left the forest behind us and were approaching the first village, he brought the car to a sudden stop. We were parked on a little, narrow bridge spanning a small, frozen brook. He grabbed me harshly and tried to pull me toward him. I pushed him away to let him know in no uncertain terms that I was not interested in his romantic overtures. When he grabbed me again, I slapped him hard across the face, opened a door, and tried to make a run for it. I only managed a few steps before he pounced on me again. We were leaning against the railing of the bridge, both of us in long Russian army coats and battling like soldiers in hand-to-hand combat. I caught him off balance and almost managed to push him over the railing, but he caught himself at the last minute and the struggle continued. Finally, realizing that I was not going to be easy prey, he ordered me back into the car, promising to take me home. He still had a tight grip on my wrist, so I had no choice but to follow his orders. We were well on our way when, in the village square, he abruptly turned the car around and headed back in the direction of the forest. I would be totally at his mercy there, with no chance of escape, and no one would hear my cries for help. I was so frightened that my eyes were beginning to sting with tears. One thing was certain though: I would fight to the very end.

Hoping that he would stop the car, I raised my foot and started pounding the dashboard with the heel of my shoes, breaking every piece of glass on the instrument panel. This did not deter him in the least. He continued to stare straight ahead, more determined than ever. As we left the outskirts of the village, the car picked up speed. If I jumped out of the moving vehicle, I risked perhaps serious injury, but there were no alternatives. It was my last and only chance to escape.

Unfamiliar with the interior of the car, I frantically searched for the handle. When he realized what I was trying to do, he reached across me and grabbed the door handle, almost wrecking the car in the process. No matter how hard I tried to dislodge his hand, he continued to hold on with an iron grip. The act of biting another human being was so repulsive to me, but as a last resort I sunk my teeth into his hand and bit down so hard that he released his grip on the handle and screamed out a few choice words in his native tongue.

In an instant, I grabbed the handle, opened the door, and jumped from the moving vehicle, landing hard on the ice-covered, cobblestone road. The heavy army coat somewhat cushioned my fall.

He brought the car to a screeching halt, missing a tree by inches. I ran to the nearest house in the hope of finding refuge there, but the house was surrounded by a waist-high wooden fence with a gate already locked for the night. Frantically, I hurled my body over the top of the fence and landed headfirst on the other side, partially blunting the fall with my hands. My head was aching as I picked myself up and raced to the back of the house. I pounded on their door and cried out, pleading for help. But before anyone could answer, I heard the soldier's footsteps coming up the path.

In a panic, I fled to a row of outbuildings in the rear of the property and took refuge in a small storage barn. The building was filled with neatly stacked rows of firewood. I listened to his footsteps as he ran back and forth, checking every building. When he reached the door of my hideaway, he cautiously inched his way into the room. My heart was in my throat. All I wanted to do was run. It was sheer agony to stand there quietly in total darkness, separated from my tormentor only by a stack of firewood. When I heard him move again, slowly closing in on me, I threw myself against the tall stack of wood with all the strength I possessed, sending it crashing down on him. I stumbled out of the building but dared not head toward the front of the house, where he had left the car with the motor running and its headlights still on. Instead, I took the back way home behind the farmhouses, where everyone was sleeping peacefully in their warm, cozy beds while I struggled through snow and ice on this so very cold night.

I continued to run, not daring to look back, trying to put as much distance as possible between us. The farmer's barking dogs began to follow me, nipping at my heels at times, but I did not mind. Their presence was almost welcome.

Hoping that I had made a clean getaway, I suddenly saw him cruising back and forth on the highway, still determined as ever to find me. Now I knew that I would not be able to take the main road home. Instead, I would have to use a little traveled back road now completely obscured by snow. The bright moonlight would help me to find my way, but it would also give my pursuer visibility for quite a distance.

As the back road branched off from the highway, there were no more trees to shield me. Instead, spread out before me was a vast white wilderness. Walking in the deep snow was difficult. The heavy Russian army coat, almost reaching my ankles, did not make it any easier, but it kept me from freezing.

As soon as I saw his headlights on the main highway, I threw myself headlong into the soft, powdery snow and stayed there until he was out of sight. Then I cautiously continued until his lights reappeared again.

I did not feel safe until I reached our village in the early morning hours. The farmers were already up milking their cows and tending their livestock, getting ready for a new day. I hoped no one would see me as I trudged through the village at this late hour dressed in, of all things, a Russian army coat. I dared not dispose of it, as warm clothing was a precious commodity those days, even for the soldiers. When the officer came back to claim it, it had better be there or there would be consequences.

I shed the coat outside the door, let myself quietly into the house, and slipped into bed without waking anyone. Mentally and physically, I was totally exhausted. When my mother questioned me the next morning, I spared her many of the details. I just told her that no harm had come to me and that I had made it safely home. My head was aching from the fall and my shoulder was bruised and sore, but soon it would heal. Erasing the memories of that night would take a little longer.

A few days later, the officer showed up at our door to retrieve his coat. He probably never learned the details of my perilous trip home. Since there was no one to complain to about this kind of treatment, we just took our lumps and went on with life.

CHAPTER 33

Most of the dance halls in the surrounding villages reopened. So on Saturday nights, we were always off to a dance somewhere. We usually went in groups, linking arms and singing along the way. Then we danced until all hours of the night and sang some more on the way home. These were simple affairs, but we did enjoy them and never got tired of dancing.

The masked balls in particular were a lot of fun. After the Christmas holidays, they were held on weekends at different villages. Since there were no store-bought costumes available, we had to be resourceful and make our own. There was so much secrecy involved in designing and making these costumes that we would not even let our closest friends know what we were going to wear. Surprisingly, despite the lack of materials, they were often quite imaginative and nice looking.

On the evening at a masked ball, the costumed participants walked in a wide circle around the dance floor while everyone else was trying to guess their identity. Once the music started, the dancing and revelry began.

At midnight, it was time for the guests to reveal their identity. They stepped onto a table set up in the middle of the dance floor and the guessing game was finally over when they removed their masks. The evening was always such fun and enjoyed by young and old.

Thus, spring passed quickly, and as May approached everyone was invited to a May Day celebration at the county seat. For the communists, the first day of May was a major holiday with many festivities, parades, and speeches. We were going more out of curiosity than to celebrate a communist holiday. Besides, they planned to slaughter several large oxen so we might as well get a good meal out of it.

We were taken in trucks and horse-drawn wagons to the site of the celebration. There were no parades but plenty of speeches extolling the virtues of communism. There were also numerous opportunities to sign up and become a full-fledged member of the Communist Party, but all of their rhetoric was lost on us. What we had seen so far of our communist conquerors did not impress us.

Chapter 34

My aunt in Berlin was doing quite well, even though it was now a divided city. Fortunately, she was living in West Berlin, which was under the control of the Western Allies. She was urging me to escape and join her to further my education, but fate interceded. While my mother and I were considering her offer, in early June of 1947, a Russian army truck came rumbling down our village street and stopped at the mayor's house. Soon the mayor with a Russian officer and two soldiers in tow were at our door. They ordered me to pack my belongings—bedding and eating utensils included—and then board the waiting truck. My mother helped me pack, insisting that I take a piece of bread and some boiled potatoes along.

My belongings in hand, I hurriedly made my way to the truck. Several other girls were already present, none of us knowing what our fate or destination would be. It was a sad departure. From the back of the open vehicle, we waved until the village and the faces of our loved ones faded into the distance.

At each village we passed through, they rounded up more girls until there was standing room only. Finally, we were on our way, heading in a northerly direction.

As darkness set in, a cold, misty rain began to fall. Soaked to the skin, we huddled close together for warmth, but a far deeper misery settled around our hearts. A soldier, apparently feeling sorry for us, reached back and handed us a large tin cup of vodka in hopes that it would help to warm us a little. It was promptly poured over the side. No matter how cold we were, we had no intention of drinking the vodka. With a thank-you, we handed the cup back to him, wishing that we could have poured his out too, judging from the way he was driving.

The heavily loaded truck was lurching from side to side, at times coming awfully close to the century-old trees that lined the highway while we were holding on for dear life. Late at night, the truck finally came to a halt beside a body of water and we were immediately transferred to a waiting ferryboat. As it carried us out into the darkness, a stiff wind was blowing, making it a very rough crossing. Some of the girls got a touch of seasickness before we reached the other shore.

Then, once again, we were ordered back into the truck to continue our mysterious journey. The night was far gone when—cold, tired, and hungry—we were ushered into a large administration building where we had to register and relinquish our identification cards. Without them, we would not be able to travel anywhere. We were beginning to realize that, until they were returned to us, we would be virtual prisoners in a forced labor camp.

We were finally released into the custody of the camp commandant who escorted us to a group of barracks nestled among trees. For the few hours of night that remained, we were assigned to temporary quarters. He issued us ration cards for the next day. Without them, we would not be able to eat. Then stating that he would return in the morning with further instructions, he took his leave.

We were so dreadfully tired that we fell asleep immediately without bothering to change our still damp clothing.

Early the next morning the camp was buzzing with activity as hundreds of girls got ready for another day of hard work. We had not eaten since noon of the previous day. After freshening up a little, we grabbed our canteens and followed the crowd to the kitchen located in another building some distance away. There we patiently waited in line until a stout and gruff older woman ladled a watery cabbage soup into our canteen. Then she handed each of us a thick, sticky slice of dark bread, which was to be our lunch. I guess there was a first for everything, but cabbage soup for breakfast?

We returned to our quarters to have our so-called *breakfast* since there were no dining facilities at the kitchen.

By midmorning, the commandant returned and assigned us to different quarters. The living conditions in this camp were deplorable. We would be housed in old, rundown barracks with broken windows and malfunctioning toilets. We also lacked the barest necessities, such as soap, toothpaste, sanitary napkins, and even toilet paper. The floors in our new quarters were dirty and littered with debris, and the only furnishings consisted of a number of metal lockers. The commandant ordered us to clean this messy room by the time he returned later in the day.

With everything in such disarray, it seemed like an insurmountable task, but we dared not complain. There were no cleaning supplies available, but we finally located an old broom. We also found some pieces of cardboard, which we used to patch the broken windows. For cleaning rags, we had to part with some of our very few pieces of clothing.

We used the metal lockers for beds, as it would be far better than sleeping on the bare floors. Placed face down, two of them pushed together made a reasonable substitute for a double bed. We spread straw, which was readily available, over the metal tops. Pillows, sheets, and blankets that we had brought from home added a little homey touch. To hold the straw together and prevent it from scattering, a sheet was spread over the top and tucked in on all sides. These were not the most comfortable beds, but we were satisfied with our effort. It was the best we could do with what was at hand.

When the commandant returned, he seemed pleased. He was a young man of slight build, perhaps in his twenties, who ran the camp with an iron fist. Surprisingly, he was not in the military. He was probably appointed to his present position because of his fluency in the German language. Everyone called him Alex. With his Slavic features and dark complexion, he looked like an Eastern European.

While he inspected the room, he scrutinized each of us intently. Then looking straight at me, he pointed his finger and announced with dread finality, "You are to be the brigadier of this group." Before I had time to inquire as to my duties, he stalked out of the room.

I was puzzled and bewildered. *Why me?* I had no political inclinations or background. I was not then nor had I ever been a member of the Communist Party. I was only eighteen and suddenly found myself in charge of up to fifty workers with no idea of what my duties or responsibilities would be. There was nothing to do but try to make the best of it. If my position would allow me to make life a little more bearable for the girls under my command, then I would certainly try.

During the day, we learned quite a bit about our new surroundings. We were on an island in the Baltic Sea. The barracks, now our living quarters, were once occupied by German soldiers. In the huge buildings that dotted the island, Werner Von Braun and his team of physicists had carried out their research and experiments. Here they had also tested and constructed the famed V-2 rockets, which did so much damage to London and other parts of Britain during the latter part of the war.

Now everything would be dismantled and shipped to Russia, even the underground water and sewer pipes plus anything else that was salvageable. Buildings that could not be moved or dismantled had to be demolished daily by use of explosives. Eventually, there would be nothing left here but a wasteland.

As evening approached, we were back in line for more soup. Apparently, this was going to be our daily diet, with cabbage soup in the morning, cabbage soup at night, and a piece of bread in between. Except for the meager food ration, there would be no compensation of any kind for our labor.

I spent a restless night not knowing what the next day would bring and whether or not I would be up to the task of leading a brigade.

The roll call was at six o'clock in the morning. Since each barrack had only one washroom, there was total chaos each morning. We stood in line for the toilet and the lavatory, wasting precious time. Then it was off to the kitchen for more soup and our small ration of bread. After hurriedly making our beds, the brigades lined up in front of the barracks. Since I still did not know what my duties as a brigadier entailed, I promptly lined up with the girls and hoped that someone eventually would enlighten me. The officer in charge soon noticed that there was a missing brigadier. After consulting with Alex, the camp commandant, he walked over, pulled me out of the line, and admonished me in a stern voice never to stand in line with my brigade but to take my position in front of them.

The first day, we were assigned to a demolition detachment. A truck carried us to one of the huge buildings on the island. Under the guidance of two demolition experts, the girls hammered and chiseled holes into the exterior walls of the building. After the dynamite was in place and the fuse ignited, we ran for our lives, ducking behind anything that offered protection. The explosion that followed shook the ground, strewing rocks and debris over a wide area.

Somehow, we all got home in one piece. There were no injuries reported. After cleaning up, I had to go to the office to obtain our ration cards for the next day. The officer sitting behind the desk stood up, shook my hand, and introduced himself as Sasha. He was tanned with a clean-shaven head and very intense dark eyes. He handed me a stack of ration cards and a worksheet on which I was to evaluate each girl's work performance. If they did not fulfill their work quota, their daily food rations would be reduced accordingly. It was my responsibility to see that this order was enforced. I was relieved when the short meeting was over. I felt uncomfortable in his presence.

The next morning when we lined up again in front of the barrack, I took my proper place in front of the brigade. Since there were no new instructions, we headed out with the same demolition team as on the previous day. Soon a second brigade arrived and, to my dismay, I learned that we were at the wrong work site. Demolition work was so dangerous that the brigades were rotated on a daily basis.

I wish my superiors had informed me of the change. Now I was responsible for idling fifty workers for a full day. Since the mistake was made, there was nothing to do but find a comfortable place and watch the action from a safe distance. We tried to cover our ears as one explosion after another shook the ground, destroying the last remnants of another era.

When I finally summoned enough courage to turn in my daily report, the officers in charge were obviously as displeased as I was. It was only my second day on the job and I had already made a big blunder. I promised myself to be more observant in the future and ask questions when in doubt. This time I was lucky and got away with only a mild reprimand.

Our new assignment involved digging and uncovering miles of water and sewer pipes, which would then be disassembled and shipped to Russia. Each day, we were accompanied by a soldier who measured out six-meter tracts for each girl, her work quota for the day. It was a hard and often dangerous task, especially if the terrain was hilly and the pipes were buried deep beneath the ground. Since we did not have the necessary material at our disposal to shore up the sides, cave-ins were a constant threat. More than once, we had to rescue a girl after she was buried by falling sand. Hardly a day went by when there was not some kind of mishap or injury.

At other times, the girls were chilled to the bone, having to stand for hours in marshes filled with cold water while trying to locate the buried pipes. Often, I would lend a hand and jump into the trench myself if the girl was simply too tired or exhausted to finish the job.

Entrance to Russian Labor Camp in Karlshagen, Germany (Usedom Island).

Russian Labor Camp Kitchen

Russian Labor Camp Assembly Area in front of barracks.

Russian Labor Camp Barracks

Russian Labor Camp Barracks

Chapter 35

One day a group of high-ranking American and Soviet officers visited our work site. We were so self-conscious of our appearance. We did not look our best with our untidy hair, sweaty faces, and dirty clothing. We wished we could hide. They were here on an inspection tour, checking out the camp and the working conditions. The Americans looked so well groomed in their handsome uniforms. *Someday,* I thought, *I might like to see this land they call America.*

I was beginning to dread the nightly visits to the office. I was always relieved when some of the other officers were present and I did not have to be there alone with Sasha. I tried my best to keep our relationship on a strictly businesslike basis, but he apparently had other plans. At his request, and with the permission of his commanding officer, he had himself transferred and put in charge of six brigades, including mine.

I knew from the onset that ours was not going to be a pleasant working relationship, especially since I continued to ignore and resist his advances. In the past, when riding to the work site, I chose to sit with my girls in the back of the truck. Now at his request I had to take a seat up front with him and his driver. We usually rode in silence to our work site, where he dropped us off, only to show up a short time later riding his horse and citing me for the smallest infractions, such as allowing the exhausted girls a few extra minutes for lunch. But worst of all were his angry outbursts when I stopped work a little too early.

Neither I nor anyone in my brigade was in possession of a watch anymore. They had been stolen from us months ago. So, at the end of our shift, I had to judge the approximate time by the position of the setting sun. On overcast days, this presented a real problem.

One night after delivering my report, I was summoned back to the office. Sasha, who had been drinking, was agitated and angry. After a harsh reprimand for stopping work ahead of time, I was banished for the night to a bunker deep beneath the ground. It was a former air-raid shelter left over from the Hitler era: a dark, cold, damp, and rat-infested hole. I was terrified but put on a good front and took the news calmly. To argue or try to defend myself would have been useless and might have even made matters worse.

Back at the barracks, I explained my predicament to the girls and then grabbed a blanket and pillow before heading out the door. To my complete amazement, all of the girls lined up behind me, each one clutching a pillow and blanket, forsaking their own comfort and safety to spend the night with me in the bunker.

As we crowded into his office, Sasha demanded that the girls return to their quarters immediately. But instead of obeying him, they locked arms and refused to budge. Fearing that he would have them forcefully evicted, I pleaded with them to please reconsider, but with a firm, "We are all in this together," they were determined to stay. The standoff continued until Sasha finally threw up his hands in utter frustration and ordered all of us back to our quarters with a stern warning that if anything like this ever happened again, there would be grave consequences. I was grateful for my brigade's loyalty, but in the future we would have to work a little longer each day to avoid another confrontation.

By now, all the girls of my brigade were on full rations, even if they were not able to fulfill their daily work quotas. When questioned about it by my superiors, I assured them that everyone performed her assigned tasks to my full satisfaction. Even on full rations, most of us were still losing weight.

After weeks on a twice-daily diet of cabbage soup, we were finally going to have a little meat for a change. But one of our girls assigned to kitchen duty cautioned us not to eat the meat. It had been delivered in nonrefrigerated trucks and was already spoiled and full of worms. So much for our special treat.

Once a woman, totally fed up with the daily diet of cabbage soup, threw the contents of her canteen at a passing Russian officer shouting, "Here, you eat this pig slop yourself." Luckily, for her, he chose to ignore her. He nonchalantly stepped over the puddle and continued on his way, his boots and uniform splattered with the smelly soup.

Life in the camp was a dull and dreary existence as we went through the same routine and ate the same food, week after week. There was no music to listen to or an occasional movie to break the monotony. In the evening, we usually found a comfortable place among the tall trees that dotted the landscape throughout the compound. We gathered wood, and then by the flickering light of the campfire sang songs, we shared our hopes and dreams for the future. Whenever soldiers passed by, we defiantly sang "The Ballad of the Cossack," a song reminiscent of the czarist era, about a faithful and loyal Cossack who swore allegiance to the czar to guard his life and his throne. Glorifying the czar did not sit well with the communists, but so far there had been no repercussions. Perhaps they did not understand the lyrics or they just chose to ignore us.

CHAPTER 36

The days began getting warmer as we approached midsummer. It was especially hard on the girls when there was no shade and they had to work out in the hot sun all day long. Without the protection of suntan lotion or any type of head coverings, many of them suffered severe sunburns. There were no salves or ointments to soothe the pain of their blistered faces and arms.

One day, it was especially hot as we loaded very large and heavy pipes, some of them two to three feet in diameter, onto railroad cars. The girls standing side by side, with their arms outstretched and the palms of their hands planted firmly against the large pipes, slowly inched it up on wooden beams and onto the bed of the rail cars. It was a tedious and dangerous maneuver, and injuries occurred daily. At day's end, almost everyone suffered from sunburns. My face was bright red and felt hot to the touch. As the night wore on, my body was wracked by chills and fever. At daybreak when I finally took a look at myself in the mirror, I was aghast; my face was so swollen that my eyes were mere slits.

For days on end, my face resembled old, cracked leather, with the skin eventually peeling off in thick layers, leaving the new, pink skin underneath more vulnerable than ever to the merciless sun.

When we were unable to go to work, we had to check in with the young Russian army doctor who had to verify that there was a probable cause for missing work. While I was in his office, he bluntly suggested that I find a virgin for him among the girls in my brigade. Somewhat taken aback by his perverse request, I promptly informed him that I would not pry into their private lives and ask such personal questions. He did not pursue the matter further, but a couple of weeks later, all the females at our camp were ordered to submit to a gynecological examination. I strenuously objected and tried to keep my brigade from having to go through this ordeal. But it was to no avail. We would have to line up with the rest of them. Perhaps his claim that he was only following orders from a higher authority to check for venereal disease was legitimate.

The camp offered very little privacy, so when I felt the need to be alone I walked down to the beach and watched the beautiful sunset with the waves of the cold Baltic Sea lapping at my feet in an endless and steady rhythm. Sometimes I stood on a bluff and scanned the horizon for signs of life. When a ship passed slowly in the distance, I watched until it was out of sight, wondering what its destination would be. At times like this, a popular song, "La Paloma," came to mind and with it an intense longing for the outside world. There was a better life beyond the horizon while I was marooned on this island for how long? No one knew.

On one of my solitary walks, I met Karl Heinz, a young man also taking a leisurely stroll along the beach. He was tall and handsome with dark, wavy hair and a very engaging smile. He and his family were allowed to stay on the island. They continued to live in an apartment complex constructed during the war to house the personnel engaged in the design and production of the various military projects, including the V-2 rockets. He was studying and planning to become an engineer. By mutual consent, we decided to meet again. Unfortunately, there was no place to take a girl on a date, so occasionally, we spent the evening walking along the beach, listening to the sound of the waves as the sun slowly disappeared beyond the horizon to mark the end of another day.

To make life at camp a little more bearable, we often amused ourselves by playing practical jokes on one another. Many an evening an unsuspecting girl would flop down on her makeshift bed and land in a cold pan of water cleverly hidden beneath the covers. With her posterior dripping wet, she tried to find the culprit. This often resulted in a chase throughout the camp. Being the leader, I was the butt of their jokes a number of times. I finally decided to take my revenge with a scheme that would affect all of them at the same time.

I asked Alex, the camp commandant, to be my accomplice. He readily agreed and showed up at our door a few evenings later. I greeted him and told the girls that he had come to make an important announcement. With both of us trying to keep a straight face, he informed them, in a solemn tone of voice, that in the near future our brigade was being transferred to a site in Siberia. We must be packed and ready at all times so we could leave on a moment's notice. It took a few moments for the words to sink in. The girls looked at each other in disbelief, and then total pandemonium broke loose. Some of the girls became hysterical, throwing themselves across their beds. Others were crying and tightly clinging to each other while the rest listened in stunned silence, too numb to speak. Never expecting such an adverse reaction, we immediately tried to put their minds at ease by telling them that they had been the objects of a joke, perhaps not a very funny one at that. But there was total chaos in the room and no one was listening. Finally, Alex blew his whistle and we got their attention. Expecting to hear more bad news, there was a sigh of relief once they learned that it was all a hoax. They were ready to kill us both for giving them such a scare. The commandant would get off scot-free, but before the week was out I was sure I would be sitting in a pan of cold water again.

Out in the field, the daily grind continued. Digging trenches day in and day out in all kinds of weather was extremely hard on the girls. Most of us continued to lose weight, as our diet did not improve. It was still cabbage soup morning and night. I was certain it would never be one of my favorite vegetables ever again.

View of the Baltic Sea off the coast of Germany

CHAPTER 37

Sasha was in charge of my brigade for quite some time now and working conditions had not improved. He continued to pursue me relentlessly. He was an individual with very intense emotions who did not take kindly to being told, "No."

One late Saturday afternoon, I was summoned to pick up my work assignments for the coming week at Sasha's quarters. He claimed to have mistakenly taken them home with him. He was my superior whose orders I was to follow. After I knocked on his door and was asked to come in, he immediately locked the door behind me. He was intoxicated and quite obviously had other things on his mind than my brigade's work assignments. When he tried to hug and caress me, I tried to push him away and a shoving match ensued. He finally became so enraged that he picked me up and tossed me like a rag doll onto his bed. Considering his violent temper, I knew then that the battle was all but lost. I was never going to leave this room until he had his way.

After being raped, I waited anxiously until he fell asleep and started to snore loudly in his drunken stupor. Ever so quietly, I got up, straightened my disheveled clothes, and after unlocking the door disappeared into the night. I ran all the way to my barracks and headed straight for the washroom, where I cleansed myself with the meager resources that were available. While most of the girls had already retired for the night, I headed without a word for my metal locker bed and lay there for a good part of the night. I was unable able to sleep as I tried to block out the past few hours. I was devastated. At the age of eighteen, I was not sexually active and the thought of an unwanted pregnancy or having a sexually transmitted disease weighed heavily on my mind.

Unfortunately, there was no one to turn to for help. The camp commandant, Alex, whom I had gotten to know very well, was a civilian and had no authority over the military personnel. The military commander would have had a good laugh at my expense if I had come to him with a complaint of a sexual attack.

Days after the assault, I experienced some discomfort in my genital area, which I tried to ignore. But the burning and itching became so uncomfortable that I finally went to the first aid station to see the young Russian doctor. It was hard to communicate with him since my knowledge of the Russian language was very limited as was his of the German language. Without examining me, he assumed that I was suffering from some type of sexual disease. For the next three days, I was to return to the first aid station and bring along a pillow. When I reported for treatment the following day, I was asked by the young doctor to lie down on one of the metal cots in the sparsely furnished room. He soon appeared with a large hypodermic needle, which he injected into a vein in my arm. After a few moments, I began to tremble and shake so violently that I was bouncing up and down on the metal cot. I lost track of time but was determined to go through with this torturous treatment if it was a cure for my ailment. I suffered through the same procedure for the next two days with the same reaction, which resembled a seizure.

But in the end, it was all in vain, as the symptoms persisted.

Russian Labor Camp First Aid Building

CHAPTER 38

One day while working in the forest, we stumbled onto a large, wooden observation tower nestled among the trees. We planned to climb it on our lunch break to see what the world around us looked like from above. But by lunchtime, most of the girls were too tired and would rather stay behind for a much-needed rest, while some of the others eagerly came along.

One after another we climbed the narrow stairs to the top of the tower, finally reaching the observation deck completely out of breath. We enjoyed a panoramic view from our perch high above the treetops.

Beyond the forest was the shoreline with the dark blue waters of the Baltic Sea stretching as far as the eye could see. Planning to play a practical joke on the girls, I suggested we shed our clothes and take a nap. All of us were soon spread out on the observation deck and enjoying the warm rays of the sun. As the girls were napping and taking a well-deserved rest, I quietly dressed, gathered up their clothes, and disappeared down the stairs. Once lunchtime was over, I called for them to come down and get back to work. Soon the girls peered over the railing, waving their arms and screaming hysterically that they could not find their missing clothes. I held them up triumphantly and told them that I would return them only if they promised never, ever to put another pan of cold water in my bed. Since they had little choice in this matter, they were only too eager to agree to my terms. When the other girls learned of our little escapade, we all had a good laugh.

Chapter 39

Since we did not receive any type of compensation, the military commander of the area decided to treat us to a dance. Perhaps he felt a little sorry for us and was trying in his own small way to reward us for the hard labor we endured.

A professional band from the mainland was scheduled to play for the coming weekend. We were so excited. We had not heard music or been to a dance for quite some time. My anticipation was overshadowed by the fact that Karl Heinz, whom I had grown very fond of these past weeks, would not be at the dance.

One night, while taking a stroll along the beach, Karl Heinz suddenly found himself face-to-face with Sasha and his cronies and was subjected to a terrible beating. Somehow, Sasha must have known that we were seeing each other and, being insanely jealous, this was his way of retaliating. Fearing for Karl Heinz's safety, I would not see him again.

As Saturday night approached, the girls began to primp, doing their hair and deciding on what to wear. We had few choices. There were no fancy dresses or high-heeled shoes. We would have to be content with the best of our work clothes.

The building where the dance would take place was in walking distance. Wide steps led up to a large hall on the first floor, where Hitler gave some of his fiery speeches during the war.

When we arrived, we found it very amusing to see some of the male musicians wearing a touch of makeup. Even the women in our village did not use makeup for fear of being labeled as "loose women."

As the music began to play, some of the officers and men were clustered in groups around the dance floor while the girls enjoyed a great time dancing with their fellow workers, young men who were also part of the labor force but assigned to a different camp. Ordinarily, we had no contact with them and kept strictly to ourselves.

I was waiting with the girls of my brigade to go in and join the merriment when Sasha suddenly pushed through the crowd and demanded, in a very authoritative voice, that I report to his room immediately to pick up the work assignment for the coming week. Unfortunately, I made the mistake once not knowing what he had in mind or what his intentions were. I was not about to fall prey to his devious and aggressive behavior again. He reeked of alcohol and was quite obviously intoxicated. I told him, "Nyet," in his native tongue and started to walk away to avoid a confrontation. Instantly he was at my side, seething with anger for my disobeying a direct order in front of everyone. He spun me around and with his right fist delivered a hard blow to my chin, sending me sprawling to the floor. Stunned, I scrambled to my feet as my girls hurriedly formed a circle around me and ushered me into the dance hall, where we tried to disappear into the crowd. I would not be able to stay. The evening I had looked forward to so much was ruined. Sasha was still guarding the front entrance, craning his neck while trying to locate me among the revelers.

Since I dared not go back to my quarters, two of my fellow brigadiers offered to put me up for the night. I was so thankful for their help, but on my account they would miss out on a rare evening of fun.

We were unable to leave through the front door so we had no choice but to make our exit through a first-floor window. It was quite a long drop down to the pavement. Standing on the ledge, we hesitated for a moment but there were no other alternatives; we would have to jump.

Fortunately, everyone survived the plunge without any broken bones. After helping each other to our feet, we ran without stopping until we reached the safety of our room, relieved to no end that we had apparently outsmarted Sasha and made a clean getaway.

One of my fellow brigadiers offered to share her bed with me, but sleep would not come. I was far too upset. So many thoughts ran through my mind. There were hundreds of good-looking girls at this camp. If I had not been a brigadier then perhaps he would not even have noticed me. I guess I would never know why he focused on me, but one thing I did know was that after this incident tonight I could not stay here any longer.

It was not fair to the girls. Not only I, but also my brigade was beginning to suffer as more and more frequently Sasha was drowning his frustration in alcohol and retaliating when I resisted his advances or refused to obey his orders. It was time for me to plan a way to escape and move on.

As the night progressed, the girls were beginning to return from the dance. One of them brought us disturbing news: Sasha was back at the camp and going from room to room, checking every bed and, in the process, waking every girl in the complex.

We were not here of our own free will. We had to live by their rules. If they chose to prowl through our barracks at night while intoxicated, we were completely at their mercy and there was nothing we could do about it.

It was time for me to be on the run again to find another hiding place. With the help of the girls, I stayed one step ahead of him. While he was searching one of the barracks, I was hiding in another. After a fruitless search through the camp, he jumped on his horse and rode like a madman out into the night.

All day Sunday he was nowhere to be seen. I was very apprehensive and dreaded the thought of eventually having to face him. Later in the day, we learned that Sasha raced to the ferry in the middle of the night, convinced that I would try to escape after he had subjected me to such harsh treatment at the dance. He remained there for the rest of the night and most of Sunday, checking every ferry leaving for the mainland.

Word spread that he was back in his quarters, somewhat subdued, and the laughingstock of the camp. Even his fellow officers were amused by his latest antics.

CHAPTER 40

Monday came and it was work as usual. Sasha made his rounds in the morning and all but ignored me. He was probably still angry about Saturday night.

My supervisory position left me with plenty of time to think. While the girls were working, I was carefully planning my escape. I would try to choose a girl with leadership ability to take my place. Hopefully, it would be a smooth transition so they would continue to get their ration cards without interruption.

On the day I planned to make my escape, they were to tell Sasha that I was not feeling well and would not be at work for a couple of days. The ferry, our only link with the mainland, was some distance away and I would have to find some form of transportation to get there. Perhaps I would be able to hitch a ride on the little train that crisscrossed the island and made a stop a short distance from our camp around nine o'clock each morning.

There still remained so many unanswered questions. Without a pass or the necessary papers, how was I going to get past the armed guard stationed at the ferry crossing? Our identification cards were never returned to us. As an able-bodied worker, and a brigadier at that, I had no hope of getting permission to leave the island. Perhaps I could sneak, undetected, or bluff my way onboard the ferry.

In the evening, after everyone had settled down, I called the girls together for a meeting and, in a hushed tone, told them of my plan. For a moment, there was silence, and then everyone started talking at once, wanting to know the details and asking numerous questions. I told them that if all went well, I would be leaving in a couple of days.

As my successor, I picked a girl named Christel. Hopefully, she would make them a good leader. She could be stern, but at the same time she was a kind and compassionate person. Any one of the girls could have turned me in to the authorities, but we always enjoyed a good and close relationship so this was the least of my worries. There had been a few minor complaints along the way, primarily over who should carry the heavy equipment to and from the work site whenever it was in walking distance. The picks and coils of rope were especially heavy and hard to carry besides their regular gear. When everyone, without exception, had to take their turn, we soon solved this problem. Before the evening was over, they all wished me well and hoped that I would succeed.

Tuesday, my final day, was uneventful. After dark, we gathered one last time around the campfire and reflected on the many experiences we shared. We tried not to dwell on the hardships we had endured but instead relived some of our happier moments with the pranks and practical jokes and the long evenings sitting under the stars, talking and laughing by the flickering light of the campfire. These were the things we wanted to remember. At my request, we sang “The Ballad of the Cossack” once more. Then it was time for the girls to turn in, for the hour was late and the fire had all but gone out; only the red embers were still glowing in the dark. I lingered a while longer, wanting to be alone with my thoughts. The camp was quiet now. Everyone had gone to sleep.

I thought of Karl Heinz and what perhaps could have been. Our paths would undoubtedly never cross again, as I had no plans to return to this island. We never even had a chance to say good-bye. I wished him well and hoped that he realized his dream of becoming an engineer.

As for Sasha, I hoped he would become a kinder, gentler person and mend his ways by realizing that you could not force your love on someone. It had to be given freely from the heart. Perhaps someday he would find the love and happiness he was so desperately seeking.

Before I called it a night, I had to dispose of my diary. I hated to part with it, but it would be far too risky to smuggle it out. During the past month, I had recorded every detail of our life at camp, including the hardships, and the happy times. Now I would have to leave it all behind. I rekindled the fire and watched as page after page was consumed by the flames until only the ashes remained.

It was well past midnight when I quietly slipped back into the room, trying not to wake the girls. In the morning, we ate our last meal of cabbage soup together. Then it was time to say our good-byes and they were off to another day of hard work.

Island railroad used for transportation from Karlshagen to ferry that runs between island and mainland.

Chapter 41

The camp was almost deserted as I gathered my belongings. I only could take a few of my things, otherwise it would look suspicious. My bedding, my eating utensils, and some of my clothing would have to stay behind. I dreaded losing any of my possessions since everything was hard to come by these days.

Having time on my hands before the nine o'clock train arrived, I nervously paced up and down the room as the minutes slowly ticked away. Finally grabbing my bag, I stepped outside and stared straight ahead. It was a beautiful, sunshiny day.

Hoping to slip away undetected, I suddenly heard someone call my name. I spun around and was face-to-face with Misha, our supply sergeant. He was a pudgy fellow with a shock of black hair and was perhaps in his late twenties. Being a brigadier, I had quite a few dealings with him in the past while securing the necessary work tools, such as ropes, shovels, picks, and axes. Often intoxicated, even on the job, his jovial personality never changed. Smelling alcohol on his breath at this early hour, a sudden thought crossed my mind. I would ask Misha to give me a handwritten permission slip so I could leave the island. He had no authority to grant my request, and hopefully it would not get him into trouble, but I was desperate and needed help.

At first he threw up his hands and would have no part of it, but when I good-naturedly dragged him by the arm toward his office and promised to return soon with a large supply of vodka, he was willing to do almost anything.

As he scribbled a few short sentences on a piece of paper, I heard the train whistle in the distance. Grabbing the note out of his hand and yelling, *"Sbasibo!"* ("Thank you!"), I headed out the door while leaving behind a perplexed Misha. I ran until I was out of breath and barely managed to make the train.

The train was almost empty with only a few soldiers and civilians scattered throughout the coaches. After a few stops along the way, we arrived at our destination. I was very apprehensive; the handwritten note was of little comfort and by no means resembled the official document required to leave the island.

There was a flurry of activity as Russian soldiers tried to maneuver several large army trucks onto the ferry, which was slowly filling up with military personnel heading for the mainland. Two young soldiers with semiautomatic rifles slung over their shoulders were checking the papers of everyone going onboard. I watched this activity from a safe distance, but I knew I must soon get in line. My heart was in my throat as I inched my way up the gangplank toward the checkpoint, trying hard to conceal my fright while trembling within.

Acting as nonchalant as possible, I handed the first soldier my little slip of paper. He looked at it with a puzzled expression on his face, turned the note sideways, then upside down, and finally handed it to his partner who went through the same motions. Neither one of them knew what to make of it, and it was obvious that both of them did not know how to read. They probably could tell that it was written in their native language, since the letters of their alphabet were quite different from those of the western European countries. They looked at me and then at the note while I stood frozen on the spot, and they never asked to see my identification card or pass. After a short discussion, they returned the note and waved me aboard.

I hurriedly ducked into the crowd of passengers consisting of military personnel with a few civilians scattered throughout. When the motors below deck finally sprang to life and the ferry eased away from the dock, I breathed a sigh of relief.

As we headed out into the open water, I took one last look at the island. I was filled with sadness for having to leave the girls behind. I would miss them. Through good times and bad times, laughter and tears, we forged a special bond. I would miss sitting around the campfire at night, the singing and camaraderie. For most of us, it was a last good-bye, for we would never meet again.

I really did not have time to indulge in such sentimental thoughts, for there were some very difficult problems facing me. For instance, how was I going to get home? There was no public transportation of any kind, and, besides, I did not have the money to pay for it. It was scary to be so far away from home, totally without funds and having to rely only on my own ingenuity or the kindness of strangers.

Perhaps some of the Russian military trucks were heading my way and I could hitch a ride before anyone realized that I had escaped from the camp. The first truck driver I approached was not going in my direction. After two more attempts, I finally found an officer and two men who were on their way to Berlin and were willing to take me along. Their route would take me to within several miles of my village.

Once the crossing was completed, I hopped on the back of their truck and found a place among some military equipment and barrels of fuel. The trip was continuously interrupted as they stopped at farms along the way, hoping to trade household goods and clothing for food and alcohol. The farmers were reluctant to part with their own meager supplies, so it was on to the next farm.

After several unsuccessful stops, the officer finally managed to talk a farmer out of a large sack of potatoes and some onions. I felt uncomfortable in the company of soldiers. Wherever we went, people would stare at me, probably wondering what in the world this German girl was doing in the back of a Russian army truck.

It was pitch dark and the hour was late when I finally reached the place where I had to get off and continue on foot in a different direction. A tap on the cab window signaled the driver to stop. I gathered my belongings and thanked them for the ride as I jumped off the truck. They were soon on their way, while I was left standing near a pub on the side of the road.

My village was still several miles away and I dreaded the thought of having to walk home alone in the dark of night. My path would take me along a highway that was primarily used by Soviet military vehicles. For a girl, it would be very foolish to walk alone along this stretch of highway in the middle of the night. To reach my village, I would also have to use a little-traveled country road that branched off from the highway.

While I was still contemplating my next move, the door of the pub swung open and several customers emerged. Among the patrons ready to call it a night, I recognized Herr Sternberg, a kindly old gentleman from our village who occasionally pedaled his bike to the pub for a few drinks and an evening of conversation. I was so glad to see him. Now I would not have to walk home alone. He was also surprised to see me and readily agreed to accompany me safely home. Along the way, we caught up on all the latest news before he dropped me off at my front door.

I was home at last, but this would never be home again. My mother, aroused from her sleep, was startled to see me. But her joy was short lived once she learned that I had not been released but instead had escaped and was now a fugitive. We both knew that I would not be able to stay. It would be only a matter of time before the soldiers came looking for me.

We decided it was best that I take the first train out in the morning and try to make it safely to my aunt's home in West Berlin and freedom. I would think about the details in the morning. I was far too tired. It had been a long, stressful day.

At the first light of dawn, I freshened up a little and, after a quick breakfast, we were on our way to the train station. It was hard to say good-bye to my family once again. As we parted and with tears in her eyes, my mother whispered, "God be with you." Both of us knew that life would never be the same again.

As usual, the train was overcrowded, but I managed to squeeze into a seat after several passengers moved a little closer together. Soon the conductor gave the all-clear signal and we slowly pulled out of the station; the steam engine huffed and puffed as it slowly picked up speed and settled into a steady rhythm.

As the train snaked through the countryside, past villages and farms, rolling meadows and brooks, I took little notice of the passing landscape. My mind was far away. What would I do? Once we reached the outskirts of Berlin, there would be pass control, and without any type of identification I would be detained until they established my identity. If I was caught, I was certain there would be some sort of punishment. I might even wind up back at the labor camp.

Freedom was so near and yet so far away.

Still crowded, the train continued to head south with passengers getting on and off at stations along the way. At midday, people were unpacking the lunches they brought from home. The lady sitting next to me offered me a part of her sandwich, but I thanked her and declined. At any other time, I would have welcomed something to eat, but at the moment I could not swallow a bite.

My thoughts began to drift back to my childhood and the many trips I had made along this very same route. But it was quite a different scenario then. Instead of being anxious and fearful, I was in high spirits and full of anticipation, looking forward to the visits with my aunt. No matter how many times I made this trip, as a child from the country there always were new and exciting things to discover in the big city of Berlin. There were trips to the zoo and to the Wannsee, a large lake on the outskirts of the city. We would take a boat tour and then conclude the day by having refreshments on the terrace at one of the many restaurants that lined the shore. There were day trips to Potsdam for a tour of the palace where German royalty once resided and held court. We would take in the latest movies and attend a concert at the Berlin Philharmonic. We would pack a picnic lunch and enjoy a day of wandering through one of the many beautiful parks scattered throughout the city. The food always tasted so good after a long walk while the birds were serenading us with their songs. Unlike today, the world then seemed so perfect, so complete.

It was all so incomprehensible how one man could lead a highly civilized nation astray and cause its total destruction. It was a civilization where the arts once flourished, a nation that was the birthplace of such famous poets as Schiller and Goethe and such renowned composers as Mozart, Beethoven, and Bach. They enriched our lives with their timeless music. Their legacy would live on for centuries to come while the legacy of Hitler and his Third Reich would forever be remembered as a time of infamy.

After hours of traveling, I was beginning to recognize some of the familiar landmarks as we reached the outskirts of Berlin. At the next station, there was the usual hustle and bustle as people, loaded down with baskets and other luggage, were shoving and pushing to get on and off the train.

Then suddenly, above the noise and confusion, I heard soldiers' voices as they entered our coach from the rear. My first inclination was to run, but I told myself that I must stay calm. I had come too far to let it all slip away and start to panic. Instead, I slowly left my seat and headed toward the small restroom. Once inside, I quietly closed the door and leaned against it, a prayer on my lips. I had to leave the door unlocked. If the sign outside the door read, "Occupied," then they undoubtedly would have checked the restroom.

With each passing moment, their voices and heavy footsteps were coming closer. They were gradually working their way toward the front of the coach, announcing repeatedly, "Pass control. Have your passes ready for inspection." The thought of being discovered was so terrifying that I had to sit down for a moment to calm my nerves. I anxiously waited and listened until they were well past the restroom before I dared take a peak outside. With their backs turned toward me, they continued to check the identification cards of the remaining passengers in our coach. I quietly slipped out of the restroom and headed back to my seat.

With trembling hands, I picked up a newspaper a passenger had left behind. I unfolded and buried my face in the paper, pretending to read. Suddenly I heard those dreaded footsteps again. Before leaving the coach, the soldiers decided to check the now occupied restroom. In a loud voice, they demanded, "Open up! Pass control." A middle-aged matron opened the door and peered out at them. She became quite indignant at having been disturbed. She began to complain loudly at the intrusion and for having to show her pass again. The soldiers paid little attention to her angry outburst. They checked her papers and, after a curt "Thank you," left the coach.

I breathed a sigh of relief. The journey filled with fear and anxiety was finally ending.

As the train headed toward the heart of the city and freedom, I thought of my family and the friends I had left behind. The land I loved was no more. Our way of life was gone forever. There would be new beginnings with some adjustments to be made as I stepped into a new and different world. It would be a world of bright lights and laughter, with food so plentiful that I would never be hungry again.

The last few years were a true test in human endurance and survival. I experienced hunger and a range of emotions from anger to utter despair and greater fear than I thought was ever possible. But thanks to God, to whom I turned in my most desperate moments, I was still whole in body and mind. Was it destiny or just circumstance that cast us in these different roles?

I harbored no ill will toward anyone. These were trying times for all of us, the enemy included. Our journey through life is but a short one. What a wonderful world this would be if all of us could live in peace and harmony instead of inflicting such untold cruelties on one another.

The past I could not change, but the future was mine to do with as I chose, for I was free at last.

Epilogue

After successfully escaping from behind the Iron Curtain at the age of eighteen, I tried to leave the memories of my terrifying teenage years behind me. It was by no means an easy choice to leave friends and family to start a new life in an entirely different environment. For fear of being apprehended, I left with few worldly possessions, but as I walked through the streets of Berlin, it felt exhilarating to be free and safe at last.

I was fortunate that my favorite aunt, Tante Lieschen, lived in the American sector of the city. Otherwise, I would have been assigned to one of the refugee camps for escapees from behind the Iron Curtain. It was late evening when I finally arrived at my aunt's apartment. She was totally surprised but overjoyed to see me and welcomed me with open arms. In the days that followed, she took complete charge of my life by first enrolling me in a business college.

Being a little on the stout side, she took some of her better dresses to a seamstress and had them altered to fit me. Because I also needed shoes, she took an expensive piece of jewelry to one of the thriving black markets and exchanged it for two pairs of shoes: high heels for eveningwear and low heels for my commute to the college every day. Tante Lieschen had a good eye for sizes and, without my even trying them on, the shoes were a perfect fit.

I made friends easily and loved the big city life. In the late forties Berlin was an exciting place to be. After almost being completely destroyed during the Second World War by numerous bombing attacks and the Soviet invasion, the transformation in four short years was truly amazing. Shops, opera houses, cabarets, movie theaters, and dance halls had all reopened and were doing a booming business.

In the hustle and bustle of this big city, I met my future husband purely by chance. I had gone out for the evening with a girlfriend. As we stood on the sidewalk to say our good-byes and were about to part, a car pulled up. Two young men with obvious American accents asked us for directions. Somehow we managed to communicate, though they spoke little German and I tried out the English I had learned at school. The handsome young man behind the wheel caught my eye, and when he asked me out on a date for the following evening, I accepted. Ordinarily I would never have gone out on a date with a total stranger, but he was so polite and well mannered that I threw all caution to the wind and actually looked forward to seeing him again. I had been dating on and off but was not quite ready to settle down into a serious, long-term relationship.

Since we were in the midst of a very cold winter, I decided to dress warmly for my date. I chose a wool sweater, a wool skirt, and a heavy coat, not knowing that my date had purchased tickets to the performance of the opera *Carmen*. After arriving at the opera house, I saw that most of the ladies were decked out in beautiful evening attire while I felt totally out of place and sat through the entire performance with my heavy coat on. We saw each other a few more times before he had to return to his office in Frankfurt. The last evening we spent together, he apologized for not being able to get me fresh flowers in the middle of winter and handed me three beautiful porcelain roses instead.

In the meantime, I learned quite a lot about his past. His name was John, but most of his friends called him Jack. During World War II, he had served in the army signal corps, attaining the rank of captain, and was in the first group of American military personnel to arrive in Berlin in August of 1945. Working with the office of the military government, he assisted in the reorganization of Germany's civilian communications system as assistant chief of the rates and finance branch. Since everything had been totally destroyed during the war, he was responsible for the reestablishment of the German postal services and international telephone and telegraph rates between Germany and other foreign countries. He also served as an American delegate who met weekly with his British, French, and Soviet counterparts at the Allied Control in Berlin to help resolve some of the conflicts created by the Soviets on a regular basis during the Cold War.

If he had a lot of meetings scheduled in the coming week, John would stay at his residence in Berlin over the weekend. We wined and dined at some of the finest restaurants, went to the theater and the opera, and danced the night away to the music of Glenn Miller. It was the best of times for both of us. What an unbelievable turn my life had taken in such a short period of time, from the harsh conditions at the labor camp to being courted by a handsome, eligible bachelor. From the very beginning, we were in a committed relationship.

In the summer of 1951 we planned a trip to Italy. Our first destination was Milan, where we danced under the stars at a garden party. We went to see the Leaning Tower of Pisa and traveled to Venice, where we rode down the Canal Grande in a gondola and enjoyed the nightly concerts at the Plaza San Marco.

On the last evening, as we walked along the Canal Grande, we saw wide stairs leading right down to the water's edge. Being in an adventurous mood, we naturally had to try them. Halfway down the stairs, our feet suddenly went out from under us and we slid very unceremoniously into the water. How romantic! Here we sat in the middle of Venice, submerged to our waists in water and covered with green slime. Apparently, the outgoing tide had left a slippery residue behind. We quite obviously were the object of snickers and stares from passersby as we made our way back to the hotel. Thus ended our vacation on a somewhat funny note.

In the meantime, our relationship had progressed to the point where we were seriously thinking of getting married. After one of his trips to Switzerland, he surprised me with a beautiful golden watch and two diamond rings. Our wedding was planned for the summer of 1951. Unfortunately, our families could not join us for this special occasion. My family was still behind the Iron Curtain, and his parents were up in age and unable to travel such a long distance. On August 10 we were married by a justice of the peace in Frankfurt, Germany, and our wedding reception was held at beautiful Kronberg Castle.

John unfortunately had to resign from the job he loved and return to the United States because he was now married to a German citizen. He had several job offers in Washington, DC, but chose instead to return to Florida, where he had been raised and had family and friends to welcome him home. He became a successful businessman who operated his own supermarket and convenience stores. I became a stay-at-home mom, raising three girls and two boys over the years. It was a busy life with me running in all directions to soccer, baseball, and karate practice for the boys and ballet lessons for the girls.

Life has been good, but at times it takes some strange twists and turns. Just a chance encounter on a street in Berlin changed the course of my life in such unforeseen ways.

About the Author

Ingeborg E. Ryals was born in Berlin, Germany, where she eventually met her American husband who after World War II was responsible for restoring the postal and telephone service. After their marriage at Kronberg Castle, they settled in Florida where they raised their children and ran a successful grocery business.

CPSIA information can be obtained at www.ICGtesting.com
Printed in the USA
LVOW040735300912

300882LV00001B/28/P